This edition first
published by Accent Press Ltd – 2009

ISBN 9781906373627

First Published by Allison & Busby 1999

Printed and bound in the UK

Cover Design by Red Dot Design

CONTENTS

Planting loose ends. Too rigid planning. Rejecting the obvious for the unusual. Controlling the plot.

9 Dissecting the Novel   119

Writing about what I know. A place called STOP. The vague plot outline. Using your library. Choice of main characters and names. Where to begin? Laying clues. The other characters. Scope for surprises. Throwing curves. Lightening the gloom. Towards resolution. Bringing in a new twist.

10 Thinking Commercially   135

Being a page-turner. Keeping the readers reading. Who do you know best? Playing it safe. Thinking globally. Popular and saleable plots. To re-cap ...

1

INTRODUCTION

When some erudite journalist or semi-interested relative asks you what your novel is about, and your mind goes totally blank ... that's when your basic plot comes to your rescue.

If you ever had one, that is. Some people don't. Maybe they are the lucky ones. They begin with a single sentence of wonderful prose or intriguing dialogue, and the story seems to spring from that point, and flows along effortlessly. And they are few and far between in terms of successful authors.

Most of us need to plan our books, so that not only do we know where we're going, but also so that we can get our characters and events from point A to point Z, without too many useless meanderings along the way.

I'm not going to give you a posh dictionary definition of a plot. You can look that up for yourself. And if you are interested in writing novels at all, you will know what I'm talking about. But to make it absolutely clear, and in its simplest terms, plot equals story, okay?

In any case, aside from its usefulness in planning a novel's progress, the word 'plot' can have several meanings. It can be a sinister and threatening word, with undertones of blowing up the Houses of Parliament. It can be a means of detailing a course of action or of mapping out compass points. It can be a devious and ruthless way of ousting members of a society. But that's not what we're concerned with, and a writer's requirements for a plot are somewhat different.

Theme, synopsis, blurb

The new writer can be confused and mystified by the words 'theme', 'synopsis' and 'blurb'. In fact, they can all be called variations on a ... well, a theme. All these things, and many more, will be included within the plot outline, and need clarifying to those who have not come across them before in a publishing context.

Theme sounds very grand, but to me the theme of a novel is merely the basic concept that the story hinges on, the starting-point.

The theme may be one of revenge, or girl-gets-boy romance, or kitchen-sink drama, or a crime of passion, or ... well, you get the picture. It can be summed up in a single word or phrase. We're not talking about filling in yet.

But to whet your appetite, many themes can be allied to such well-known proverbs as 'blood is thicker than water' (a sibling power-struggle novel, perhaps), or 'better the devil you know' (could this be marrying the wrong man?). In using a proverb or well-known cliché as your theme, the possible choices would be many. There will be more detail about theme in Chapter 2.

The **synopsis** is a much sharper, shorter précis of the entire plot. It is your selling tool that you offer to a publisher, with or without the first three chapters of your book, or sent with the entire novel. Its purpose is to inform publishers not only that you are about to write a sparkling novel that they cannot afford to bypass, but also that you have the wherewithal to create a solid plot. The finer points of the synopsis will also be dealt with in a later chapter.

The back cover **blurb** is usually the publisher's province, and not yours. It is used to show the reader briefly what the story is about and to entice the reader inside. On hardback books, especially, there is usually an inside front cover blurb as well, which may be different from the back cover, and which you may or may not be asked to write yourself. This depends on the publisher's quirks and need not concern you until or unless asked for it.

Both these blurbs differ from the synopsis, because they tease the reader with the contents of your novel, whereas the synopsis *per se* leaves the publisher in no doubt how you have shaped and planned your plot.

If you are invited to write your own inside front cover blurb, don't be modest about the strength of your story and the passion of your characters. As this will eventually be printed for the readers' benefit, let everyone reading it see that you really care about your characters and story, even if in as little as 200 words, which is often all that is required. This may horrify you, and it is really paring down the plot and the synopsis to its bare bones, but it is also a useful exercise in cutting, while not giving too much away.

You are not explaining to the *publisher,* in this instance, what your book is about. By the time you have been asked to write your inside front cover blurb, you should have a contract in your hands, so you can afford to be confident about its future. The lure of the inside front cover blurb is to tempt the reader into wanting to read this book above all others. When you consider the mass of books on any bookshop's shelves, it's no time to be modest about your book's content.

Are you a plotter?

Regardless of all the other meanings of the word 'plot',

we writers have a far more innocent reason for using it. The plot of a novel details your characters' journey through the pages. It is not just what happens in a given time-slot. It's also what your characters do, and how they behave and interact, that all goes towards making your invented story believable.

So, a few introductory words about your characters before dealing with them in depth. The most successful writers are those who can create believable characters who live and breathe off the page. Fictional characters have a great advantage over real-life people, because, we, their creators, can make them do anything we want them to.

We can make them change their minds at will, give them whatever good or bad traits we choose, dictate when they will be born and marry and die. We can give them whatever horrendous diseases we wish (even invent a few unknown ones with no known cure), we can cherish our heroes and heroines, and kill off the villains when they have outdone their usefulness. We are akin to the age-old tradition of Eskimos, in that we put out our old and infirm to die ...

These are reckless statements, perhaps. But the system works, providing we have planned well enough to make such events logical, and not so far-fetched as to bring your manuscript winging back to you by the next post. I will repeat a phrase I always quote when I'm talking to writers' groups: write visually; think logically. It has always stood me in good stead.

Spontaneity

The apparent loss of spontaneity in plotting a novel in detail really worries some people who believe that simply by writing things down in a sequential manner you will lose the spark of that so-called muse. The simple answer is that you won't lose it at all. Why should you, when you can always change your first thoughts, or your tenth? A flash of inspiration to put new life into a flagging scene isn't taboo just because you have outlined things methodically.

I hardly think anyone would disagree that the late Nicholas Monsarrat was a successful author whose books flowed effortlessly. Yet he was reputed to have said that when he began writing on page 1, he knew precisely what would be happening on page 286. That's methodical for you – and it's taking plotting to extremes by most people's standards.

It also sounds like a lot of hard work ... so let's be more realistic. Looking at it objectively, you may well discover that plotting and planning can be lovely words to a writer who hasn't yet begun the hard work of actually *writing* the novel. Because you're still playing around with ideas. You're somewhere in dreamland, that lovely airy-fairy state when you know there's a book in there somewhere, and you only have to work things through ...

Even in that happy state, you're really working, of course, and you're telling yourself that this is essential stuff and not time-wasting. It's all perfectly true, as long as you don't spend so much time planning that you never get down to writing the novel at all. This also goes for research.

There comes a point when enough is enough, and you need to begin, to see that novel start to take shape, and to breathe life into your characters and their story. You won't do that while your thoughts are all in some haphazard and jumbled state and your desk is hidden beneath a delightful chaos of notes and scribbled jottings.

Clinical and sensible

Of course it's sensible to know where you're going. You wouldn't board a train without knowing your destination, and writing a novel without at least *some* idea of the end as well as the beginning makes no sense. If this is the clinical approach, so be it. Even those who say they never plot their books, and let the story take them where it will, are fooling themselves to a degree.

It's the nature of any writer to mull things over in the mind. To let the subconscious – that marvellous aid to creativity – supply the answers to tricky questions while you sleep. A great deal of the 'writing' is done in thinking or dreaming time, and it all leads you towards unscrambling the mass of ideas that you think will never turn into a publishable novel. Catherine Cookson has been quoted as spending much of her non-writing time in planning and plotting her books in her imagination, visualising the clashes between characters, 'seeing' the scenes as they unfold, and rehearsing the dialogue in her head.

There are many ways of plotting and planning a novel (or not). Conan Doyle simply imagined a seemingly bizarre or impossible situation and searched for a rational explanation that Sherlock Holmes would deduce in order to solve the crime.

Bringing us all down to earth, Agatha Christie said that the best time for planning a book is when you're doing the dishes. Which proves that even the most respected authors are human too.

So where do you begin to make sense of it all? This book concerns plotting your novel, but the characters should be very much at the forefront of your mind when thinking about your plot. These two essentials are of equal importance in creating a readable book. And what we are all striving for is to write a book that readers can't put down. Just as importantly, since we're in business and publication is our aim, we want to write a book that has editors reaching for their cheque books.

Character

Every novel involves characters. Without characters you have no story. However wonderful your background, however descriptive and lyrical your writing style, however meaty your intricate historical battle scenes, however complex and mind-breaking your mystery or crime novel, none of them works without realistic characters leading the reader through the pages. They are, in effect, telling their story, the one that you have planned and devised for them.

And what that reader finally wants to know is how your sleazy detective turned out to be a hero in disguise. How the heroine with everything to lose got her man. How such fantastically ludicrous character-led plots could become as addictive to readers as Terry Pratchett's *Discworld* novels.

So, disregarding for a moment the fact that you have to have characters to people your novels, the first essential is plot. The second is comeuppance. Think about it.

Every novel you ever read has that sweet satisfaction of good triumphing over evil, or the baddie getting his just deserts, or some clever twist proving the central character's worth. Even those dreary kitchen-sink dramas have *some* element of hope and resolution beyond the final pages. And did·this all happen accidentally? Of course not, unless you're one of the few-and-far-betweens already mentioned.

Most of us work very hard to make the simple appear

complex. We strive to put unexpected twists and turns in the story to ensure that it doesn't flag. We aim for surprises, within the context of keeping our characters true to themselves. We create as sound a plot as we can before we even begin Chapter 1. Don't we?

Confession time

And now it's confession time. No, I'm not one of the few-and-far-betweens, who are going to become clichés if I'm not careful, so I won't mention them again. But I am a plunger. I'm impulsive. I plunge right in the minute I've got an idea in my head, and get something down on paper, or rather on screen. Something to get my teeth into, even if it's only that dramatic first sentence of dialogue, or that all-important first scene on page 1.

Sometimes I have written as much as two or three chapters before I tell myself to stop, and practise what I preach. Another cliché, but it's pretty useful to have a ready-made phrase that says exactly what you mean. In moderation. And yes, I *know* I have to have a plot to work to in the end, because that's the best way I know to get my novels to unfold naturally.

So why do I work the way I do, and frequently find myself writing out a detailed plot when I've already begun my book? Doesn't this method create all kinds of problems? How can you be sure, in the first rush of enthusiasm and white-hot writing, that it will all tie up with your more soberly written plot, when you don't have a gin and tonic by your side driving you along? Or in my case, usually black coffee ...

Yes, it does often cause some backtracking, but since I also believe in spontaneous writing, I feel the risk is worth it. And any writer who is a writer should be prepared to revise a couple of chapters, or even to ditch the lot and begin again. We shouldn't be so precious that we think everything we write is perfect, and that a word shouldn't be changed. Far from it.

If that's your attitude, you're in danger of being shaken, if not badly stirred, depending on your publisher, to find that your wonderful prose can be torn to shreds by a ruthless sub-editor. Even copy-editors can tinker with your grammar – and sometimes change the whole meaning of a sentence and alter your writing style in doing so. Believe me! Let them know your feelings if that happens, as I have done.

But once you've got over the hurdle of accepting that somebody else is eventually going to have more than a hand in your work, one of the best things about writing is to realise that nothing is written in stone or in blood, and you can always change things, move characters around, sharpen weak scenes, expand or condense where necessary. You are in control. It's your book. It's your story. It's your plot.

The point I'm making here is that every writer's method is his or her own. I don't always work the way I have just outlined. There have been times when I've submitted a chapter-by-chapter breakdown of my books to an American publisher, because that's the way they wanted it. I found it a pretty nerve-racking way of working, frankly, but the book was incredibly easy to write – as far as any book is easy to write – once I had chuntered my way through the chapter-by-chapter breakdown. I could 'see' the entire plot so clearly, and knew where the weak spots were, and where I needed to strengthen them.

I have since discovered that I was in good company. John Braine said he initially made a chapter-by-chapter plan of his novels, and so did Arnold Bennett.

There was one occasion, and only one, when I 'dreamed up' the entire plot of a short contemporary novel on a coach coming home from London, and wrote the book in ten days with only the sketchiest plan on paper, and most of it in my head. (Not to be recommended unless you enjoy mental exhaustion.)

A plot notebook

It's useful to keep a plot notebook in which you jot down all kinds of possible ideas that may or may not go into the making of an eventual novel. Into this notebook may go possible titles – and don't scoff at the thought that you could concoct an entire plot from an inspiring and an evocative title.

You may know the hymn that begins with the line 'All in the April Evening'. It has a haunting tune that I seem to have always known. A twist on a recognisable phrase will attract readers, which is how I came to call one of my novels *All in the April Morning*. For the title to have any significance, I decided that everything of importance in my central character's life, whether good or bad, should happen during any April morning. It was a novel that covered many decades, and the realisation of the April trauma gave depth and strength to the character. That's how it worked for me.

Your notebook could also carry ideas of certain occupations, locations, battles, important moments in history, national and international events, political or sporting figures who interest you, and so on. I have always kept a notebook recording such things, and of my own impressions when visiting places. This makes sense to me. Jilly Cooper is known for recording scents and smells, and relevant flora and fauna wherever she goes. This is a good tip to follow, so that you don't have daffodils blooming in October ...

Speaking personally

I have published dozens of novels now, and every plot is different, depending on the vast choices that every author has in devising a plot. Yet I still vary my actual writing methods according to my mood and the requirement of the publisher. So my advice is don't be hog-tied by any restrictions that will block the creative flow.

Writer's guides, such as this one, are intended to be of help to beginners, and I think of them as an instant dipping-into refresher course to old hands. If something that you read is against everything you want to do, then once you have absorbed the advice and considered it, you are perfectly at liberty to ignore it. But do consider it.

Writing is a personal occupation, and everyone has their own preferred method of going about it. It's what makes us all individual. Rona Randall is an author who says she does little initial plotting. She says that trying to fit characters into a preconceived plot never works for her.

Alan Sillitoe says he is content to write an opening line and see where it leads him. Wow! Monica Dickens, too, when asked if she knew the ending to her novels before she began, said that she simply puts down the central characters, and then follows them. I suspect that Joe Bloggs, doing the same thing in these highly competitive and commercially orientated days, would still be unpublished ...

So you make your choice. One thing is for sure, and that is that you must love the work you do, and revel in sorting out the lives and fortunes of the characters you

11

create. I have never subscribed to the 'lonely life' you're supposed to lead. If you're doing a job that you really love, solitude is one of the things that makes writing possible. Feel lucky if you have it, and cherish it. Not everyone has that luxury.

And it really doesn't matter whether you take a day or a month or a year in devising your story, or the way you go about it. Except that if you ever want to see any returns on your efforts, I'd advise you not to wait until you've got one foot in the proverbial pit before you begin.

Having got all that out of the way, there are many people who long to write a novel, convinced that they've got a book in them, but don't have a clue how to go about it – and for whom the word 'plotting' is a mysterious thing. But when all's said and done, writing is a job as well as a craft, and learning as much as you can about the mechanics of any job is part of being successful.

So for those who prefer to go about it the so-called 'proper' way (and all credit to you), this book is for you.

2

FIRST THOUGHTS

I love being a writer. What I can't stand is the paperwork
Peter De Vries

The quote from Peter De Vries must strike a chord in every beginner's heart, and make even the most accomplished professionals give a wry smile.

How *do* you begin to create something from nothing? And where do you begin? Real life is definitely a chancy affair, with no predictable plot to it at all (and how boring it would be if everything in life were so), but a successful novel knows where it's going because of its plot.

It's tidied up while not being sanitised. Surprises are there for a reason. The cast of characters, whether large or small, are as interwoven and as essential to the plot as any cast of characters in a play. The shape and movement of the story will depend on what kind of novel it is, but it must *have* that shape and movement, or everything will remain static. If that is so, then by the time readers reach the last page, if they get that far, they will start to ask themselves what it was all about. This is fatal.

Just as your characters must have motivation for their actions (or what are they doing in your story at all?), so the novel must have a purpose, and that purpose is what drives the plot forward.

It's not much good deciding grandly that you are going to write a novel if you don't have a clue about the kind of novel you want to write, or have no idea of how the forward thrust of such a story will progress. Preferably it will involve something you feel passionate about, something that you have a burning need to get down on paper at all costs.

So we're back to theme again. Maybe you feel that a deep social problem, such as the homeless in our inner cities, is a worthwhile theme that you could write about. Or you badly want to write a crime or adventure novel, and feel the urge to create your own Morse, or Wexford, or James Bond. There's nothing wrong in that, and new crime detectives are always springing up for an apparently insatiable readership.

But do think hard about the fictional characters you most admire, or you may end up writing facsimiles of these well-known characters, and no publisher will risk buying a novel that depends too strongly on those who have gone before. You will certainly not want to be accused of plagiarism.

I'm not saying that you cannot create another magnificent fictional crime solver, or seducer of bountiful ladies while seeing off heinous villains. Just that you should concentrate on creating your own characters, without relying heavily on other people's. Admire them, by all means, but be as original and inventive as possible.

Similarly, try to develop your own style. When I began writing historical romances I was once asked by a snippy radio interviewer if I wanted to be another Barbara Cartland. My equally snippy reply was that I wanted/intended to be the first Jean Saunders.

It doesn't necessarily do a writer any good to be described as the new whoever, however wonderful you may feel at the time if an agent, editor or reader says that your book reminds them of so-and-so ... We've all heard that kind of thing before. Some authors have even been written up on the jackets of their books as being the new ******** ... And I'm not risking anything by naming anybody here!

The initial idea

Every plot comes from an initial idea that may be as ephemeral as a summer breeze. The idea can come from practically anywhere. It can be caught from an overheard conversation – especially when you hear only half of it – or a newspaper item, or a scene in a play, or a currently hot political drama, or the agony pages of a magazine. If you think that authors don't seize on these moments, and these wonderful sparks to set them off, then you're living in a dream world.

But the idea, the spark, is only the beginning of what you hope will evolve into a book. There's a long way to go between that idea and a finished work that may be anything from 55,000 words long to 150,000 words or even more, depending on the type of novel you want to write.

Ideas are infinite and everywhere. Anyone who says they can't find one, simply isn't looking, or listening. So let's think of an imaginary scenario. Let's say that you want to write a romance about a girl who wants to get away from an unhappy situation at home, who applies for a job as far away as possible from everyone who knows her. This is the basic idea, and it could be any kind of job, from a deep-sea diver to a courier. Obviously it is also an ideal situation for a romantic novel.

Write about what you know

You will almost certainly have heard or read the advice

that you should always write about what you know. This advice is good, but it is only half true. Writing about what you know is wise – especially for a new writer – but if you don't know enough about a certain subject or a background that really interests you, then find out, so that you can then write with confidence and authority. (More about this in Chapter 6.)

All of us know something about love, in some form or other. This is the most basic emotion of all. Love comes in many guises other than the romantic – from tender to raunchy to erotic. Love can be for a child, parent, pet, sibling, husband, lover ... So let's get back to our imaginary scenario and pretend that our fictional girl has been thwarted in love. Needing to get away from all that's familiar to her and nurse her wounded pride, she replies to an advertisement to act as secretary to a writer on a remote Scottish island.

Well, you know something about writers, don't you? You *are* one, after all, whether you're still aspiring to be published, or well established. And presuming that you may have once worked in an office – or been in enough of them over the years, for whatever reason – then you either know, or can make a shrewd guess, at a secretary's duties. So far, so good.

Shall we let her get the job? If we don't, your story is going to end pretty quickly. So she gets it. And yes, her boss is predictably dishy, and they eventually fall for each other. Bingo. Beginning and ending. Plot complete. But hey, there's a long way to go between the initial idea and a likely 55,000 word journey towards that ending.

The idea *is* just the beginning. It has to be nurtured as carefully as a tender seed; questioned, built upon, rejected, and finally sorted through into some kind of logical pattern before a full-blown plot makes the whole thing feasible.

Guilty, m'Lud ... yes, the above idea was one of my own, and it resulted in my first romantic novel, *Ashton's Folly* (writing as Jean Innes). As a first-time novelist after many years of successful short-story writing, I threw everything into it: missing children; subplots galore; thwarted love affairs; and more than one attractive man to confuse the issue ...

The original plot was an endless ramble, and it needed considerable reorganising before I was happy with it, but I had stumbled on a secret that I have since found useful. If you make your initial plotting as involved and detailed as you can, it's far easier to cut and refine it, than to fill in gaps which may just end up as padding. Throw in *everything,* and then be ruthless and *cut.* I also dreamed up a method of plotting that I thought was unique, but which has since been described by other writers, including Dianne Doubtfire. It was quite comforting to realise that I was not alone after all.

It's the 'numbers method'. It was crude but effective, at a time when I was undergoing the nervous transition from short-story writer to novelist, which seemed like a vast leap into the unknown to me then.

It was also incredibly simple. I numbered a page from 1 to 20 to represent chapters. Why twenty? No reason. I just picked a number, so don't get the idea that all novels have to have twenty chapters, because of course they don't. But at this embryo stage of my plot I was only sure about two things:

- I knew where my story was to start (girl planning to leave home, applying for a job, and getting it).
- I knew where the story had to end (girl finding true love with employer).

This was where the imagination had to come in, by filling in those other numbers (i.e. chapters), with a logical progression of events, with highs and lows, twists and turns, dramatic scenes, conflicts, doubts and indecisions...
Corny or what?

I can only tell you that it worked. The book sold to Robert Hale after the necessary hiccup of needing to shorten it to their specifications. I had overwritten, which is a basic fault of most beginners. The plot of the novel remained intact, but the necessary editing and revision tightened it up considerably, and made it a better book in the end.

Eventually, through Robert Hale's subsidiary rights department, it appeared as a *Woman's Weekly* paperback, and in hardback for a Dutch publisher. Hale then sold it as a Bantam paperback in America, UK and Australia, and in several large print editions, both hardback and paperback. It was also included in an American book club edition, and still does well in libraries, even though it's more than thirty years since it was first published.

The overriding point I can make about that book is that it had a sound plot. But one of the things I stress to anyone bewildered by the mass of advice they are given on all sides, is that whatever method of plotting works for you, *use it,* and don't let anyone tell you it's wrong.

Basic requirements

If the idea is just the beginning, then the final, detailed plot that you devise from those first thoughts is most definitely the end of the beginning. It's not the end of the book, because you haven't begun to write it yet.

But once your plot is thought through and written down on paper, you can look at it, study it, discard any false trails that hinder the forward flow of the story, and add any sudden inspirational thoughts that come to you. They will, of course, because by now your imagination is in full flow. Then you're really on your way.

I will repeat a key sentence. *Get it down on paper.* It's amazing how alive your vague ideas will look when they're in written form. You have something concrete in front of you. You can see the shape of things to come; the final story will begin to emerge from that jumble of thoughts that you never thought would form a plot, let alone a published book.

In this context, the novelist Jean Rhys says that a novel has to have shape, and that life doesn't have any. One of the most useful things about plotting your novel is that you can see the finished shape of it before you actually begin writing. You can see if you are sticking to your original plan, and you can discard any sidetracking that impedes the forward progression of the story.

Every novel has a certain shape to it. It may start off slowly, while the characters and setting are defined, but then it gathers momentum and intensity as it moves ahead towards its conclusion. Think of an imaginary diagram – or sketch out a real one – of a rising graph with minor peaks and troughs before you reach this conclusion, which will give you the shape of your plot. Or, once you have plotted your story in sequential form, you might even think about sketching a diagram at that stage, to see if it conforms to the necessary peaks and troughs that you envisaged.

Many people have brilliant ideas, but they are tenuous, and they do not have the shape or form of a plot. Until you write them down, you may not even see how slight they are, or realise that they don't have the stuffing to create a real book. They may make no more than a short story, and to try to stretch a short story into book-length material rarely works.

When starting to plot your novel, be sure that you have enough solid material behind the basic idea of creating a believable fantasy world, a boy-meets-girl romance, or a super-divine hero solving the world's biggest scam.

The theme of your book

Sometimes you are unsure what your theme really is, but once you find it it will assist the way you plan and shape the book. Quite often the theme can be summed up in a single word. Perhaps your theme is 'abuse'. If you feel strongly about this subject, then your options are immense.

- Parental Abuse.
- Child-minding abuse.
- Hospital abuse.
- Wife-battering.
- Sibling or school-bullying abuse – from teachers or from other pupils. It happens.

There are infinitely more options, and any one of them can involve verbal or physical or sexual abuse. Take a little time to let your mind expand to imagine any of the above situations, and if you are anything of a fiction writer at all your thoughts will automatically move on towards how such a situation could be resolved.

Maybe your theme is the serious one of bereavement. This again is a vast area to develop. To write a novel based on bereavement, obviously someone has died, and someone else is coming to terms with it. So who has died? A child? Husband, parent, lover?

I suspect that anyone wanting to write about such a searingly sad topic will have had some experience, either in their own lives, or with someone close to them.

Now here's something you may not have thought about. It's a creepy thing for writers to acknowledge that because all experiences in life can be used as material we view everything with two sides of our consciousness.

On the one hand, we have the normal human reactions, and on the other, we mentally register everything we see and feel. I know this from personal experience. It happened to me when my mother had a terminal illness, and we had been given a time limit on her life expectations. The side of my personality that had developed through my writing was the only thing that kept me sane at such a time.

But once the inevitable guilt of knowing that I was registering everything on two levels had dissipated a little, I realized it was a wasted exercise to feel doubly anguished because I was absorbing the entire experience, feelings and emotions in this way. We're writers, and writers draw on real life and real experiences, however harrowing. Your theme is abandonment or divorce? Same thing. But let's lighten up, I hear you say. So your theme is a hijack. Well, it's a lighter topic than any of the above, for heaven's sake! Where will this take place? Think of the options.

- On an aircraft or a ship?
- In a foreign country or inner city location?
- Are we talking about a spy situation here?
- Is it a bomb threat?
- An escaping gang of prisoners?
- A ransom demand?

It's your book. You decide.

Genre or mainstream?

You should also be thinking about the type of book you want to write. Before you begin to plot the book in detail, you need to know which genre, if any, it will fit into.

It's a fine and noble sentiment to say you intend to write your own thing, and that you are a free spirit with your own unconventional ideas. Great. But if you want to be published, you'll find that most publishers put their authors and their books in certain slots. It's a selling ploy for them, and a useful guide for an author to look through any publisher's catalogue of forthcoming titles, to see the range of books listed under Crime, or Romance, or Historical, or Science Fiction, or General Fiction, and so on.

Writing is a highly competitive and commercially orientated business, and your way-out book may be too much of a risk for a publisher to take on. On the other hand, there are exceptions. *Watership Down* is a classic example. But, as a beginner, give yourself the best chance of publication by conforming to a recognised category as far as possible.

The kind of novel you intend to write will influence your plotting, partly because of the book-length, and because of the style in which you will write it. For example, a fast-moving detective story, or a multi-viewpoint blockbuster saga, will need a plot with more twists and turns and red herrings in it than a short, straightforward romance.

Think also about the type of novel you are most at home with before you think about the plot. Know what you want to write, which will probably be akin to the type of novels you enjoy reading. Or it may not. Many writers have wanted to turn their talents to writing something totally different from their regular genre.

Charlotte Lamb is a case in point. Indisputably one of Harlequin Mills & Boon's top writers for many years, she has also written historical and crime novels, while still keeping up a steady output of what her romance readers devour. Don't be afraid to spread your wings, but whatever you do, enjoy what you write. If you don't, it will show.

Choices

There is a vast choice of categories, and this is a favourite word among editors and publishing catalogues. But one thing remains constant, you'll be relieved to hear. Plotting a novel in any of the specialised categories requires the same basic needs of memorable characters moving through your planned time-slot, story-line, conflicts and soul-searching problems, with goals to reach and the motivation for reaching them.

These are just a few of the listed categories, including some of the less immediately recognised ones:

- Contemporary or historical romance.
- Political thrillers.
- Fictional 'kiss-and-tell'.
- Wartime sagas.
- Regional novels.
- Espionage.
- Erotica.
- Sex and shopping.
- Kitchen-sink dramas.
- Fantasy and science fiction.
- Horror.

To qualify the downside of suggesting that you keep to accepted categories, originals also have their place, of course: such as Helen Fielding's *Bridget Jones's Diary, The Bridges of Madison County,* Jonathan Gash's *Lovejoy* books ... medical humour, such as Robert Clifford's *Just Here, Doctor*; Sue Townsend's *Adrian Mole* books; and the massively successful James Herriot books.

Don't think that your off-beat and original story has *no* chance of finding a publisher. The main stumbling block is that it may be harder to convince him that this particular book is going to make him money as well as you, but if you have worked out a resoundingly solid plot, and have convinced *yourself* that it works, then go for it.

And be confident in your ability to write the book when approaching the publisher of your choice. If he senses that you are unsure whether or not you have a sound proposition to offer, it does not bode well for a profitable relationship.

Avoiding the formula

The formula is something you intend to avoid in writing *your* novel, of course ... but if you think of it as merely the pattern, or shape, of the book, then you will realise that there is a certain pattern in all novels. The most obvious is that there must be a beginning, a middle and an ending ... but what happens between the first page and the last, is, and should be, different in every book you read.

The most prolific authors strive to make every book different, and the most creative ones see the so-called formula as a challenge, to test their ingenuity in devising plots that still conform to the restrictions of a popular genre. 'Formula' is not a dirty word.

Romance and crime novels are the most obvious

targets for the formula slur, a tag that the more purist of the literati people attribute to the word. But what's wrong with knowing your parameters for a favourite form of writing, to which devoted readers become addicted?

Every crime novel involves a crime being committed, plenty of red herrings along the way to confuse the issue, and eventually having the crime solved by some clever-clogs female-sleuth/police inspector or his sidekick/amateur detective or private eye. And who can deny the abiding popularity of these, still essentially formula novels?

Every romance novel, from *Jane Eyre* to the contemporary chick-lit novels, has the required element of two characters who meet and fall in love, encountering and overcoming the many obstacles along the way, and eventually finding their happy ending. We should all be so lucky!

How long is a book?

The length of a book is a basic question that many beginners ask in all innocence, and should never be sneered at by more experienced authors. After all, you wouldn't know the intricacies of brain surgery without plenty of guidance and inside information ... no pun intended.

Plotting your novel depends not only on the type of book you are writing, but also on its length. This one fact alone has a great influence on whether or not your book ever gets published.

The beginner writer may naïvely think that their book can run and run until it comes to a natural ending, and its sparkling text and witty dialogue will ensure its acceptance. Not so. All publishers have a budget, and the cost of paper has become prohibitive in recent years, with the consequence that fewer door-stopper books are being published.

This has afforded some relief to those readers who found difficulty in holding the hardback edition in their hands at all, and in discovering that the paperback pages simply wouldn't stay open comfortably for bed-time reading.

It is easy enough to study the bookshop shelves to see which authors can still get away with very lengthy books, and unless you are a Melvyn Bragg or one of the top-notchers (and you will know who they are), you would be wiser to tailor your novel to reasonable lengths.

Some publishers state their required lengths in their guidelines. Again I must quote Harlequin Mills & Boon here, who give comprehensive lengths for all their lists. It's always worth contacting an editor for such information if you want to write for a specific publisher. Most are not ogres and are receptive to such requests, and infinitely prefer it to receiving totally unsuitable material.

You can also calculate the length of published novels by counting the words on a number of sample pages and multiplying them by the number of pages in the book. This is a good do-it-yourself way, if tedious. Or, if you have a kindly agent, he/she will often advise on the lengths required for a particular publisher.

To allay the rage of any agents who may be reading this book, let me hasten to say that I know this is not their prime role. But in my experience, once they have taken an interest in you and your writing, they will usually oblige with such basic information, since it will save them, and you, and the publisher, the frustration of getting it wrong.

Ideas from old sources

When your ideas seem to be in short supply, turn to those that have gone before. Your own family history, for example, may be a rich source of fiction material, providing you don't write it up as an autobiography, which tempts so many first-timers.

It's inevitable, and very seductive, to believe that our own lives are fascinating and would make a marvellous story for others to read. Maybe so, but it's far safer than having to placate any irate relatives to write it all up as fiction, using your family's history as the basis, embellishing the known events, and including far more adventurous details than actually existed. (More on this later.)

I adapted something from my own family background in one of my books, *To Love and Honour*. The facts were that one of my uncles emigrated to Australia, joined the Australian army, married and had a family there. As a child, I always found this a source of glamour, although, in effect, his life followed a very ordinary pattern of events.

Although I planned *To Love and Honour* with this in mind, by the time the plot evolved, very few of the original facts were included. In my book a brother and sister had had an incestuous relationship that produced a child – the rags-to-riches heroine of the book. The man whom she thought was her uncle had emigrated to Australia. He was, in fact, her father.

This was a world away from my family background, but the true and, to me, rather glamorous facts gave me the spark on which to hinge my fictional plot.

You could study any classic or contemporary novel and see how the plot evolved. Look beyond the story itself, and try to work out how the author put the events together that kept the story moving. It can be a fascinating exercise, and being a reader is as important to a writer as breathing – providing you don't spend all your time reading other people's books and not getting on with your own.

Summary

- The initial idea is your plot starting-point.
- Find a theme you're passionate about.
- Know the kind of book you want to write.
- Keep the proposed length within publishing bounds.

3

WHERE DO THE CHARACTERS COME IN?

The central theme is that they were glad to see each other
Gertrude Stein

Every novel needs characters in it, or it becomes no more than an essay or report. You may have heard reference to a character-driven plot, as if there is really any other kind. In my opinion, there is not. All plots are basically character-driven, because without them you have no plot at all. Characters bring your story to life.

Think about a beautiful painting that is all scenery and nothing else. However lovely, soothing or dramatic it may be to look at, it's a still-life scenario. The moment you put a person in the scene, your subconscious tells you that he or she is there for a purpose. She may be merely looking at the view, as you are, but she is using her senses – just as you are. Put several people in the scene, or a family group, and your inner imagery of these people changes. In other words, there is a story there, and you automatically accept it.

Characters are a vital part of any plot. Some while ago I was giving a talk about novel-writing, and the question being asked was about continuing with the same characters in sequels and trilogies. At that time I had just finished the fifth book in a sequence of Cornish novels set in the mid-nineteenth century that began with *Killigrew Clay* (writing as Rowena Summers). My heroine in the first book, Morwen Tremayne, was then a beautiful, fiery girl of seventeen, and worked as a bal maiden at the local china clayworks.

With the fifth book in the sequence of novels, the continuing stories had reached the First World War, and Morwen was then eighty years old and nearing the end of her life.

At the talk I was giving, I explained to my audience how difficult it was for me to think of her at that age, even though I had steered her through two lusty marriages and a clutch of children and grandchildren by then, to say nothing of the fluctuating fortunes of the china clay industry and the intricate family saga background. And how hard it was going to be for me to finally say good-bye to her.

One lady said in amazement: 'But you're talking about her as if she's real! As if she really existed!' And my answer to that was: 'Of course I am. She's as real to me as if I've known her all my life. I've shared all her joys and sorrows, and I shall weep at her death.'

For the record, I did. If you want your characters to be believable to readers, the first requirement is that all of them should seem as real to you as living people, otherwise they will simply come across on the page as cardboard cut-outs.

Memorable characters

The fact that I knew Morwen so well, and cared about her, made everything she did important to me. As the central character through all of the books, she was the pivot around whom the rest of the book flowed. Is this essential core another secret of successful novel-writing? I'm convinced that it is.

Memorable characters who stand out in novels are those who are larger than life, but who still retain the human elements with which we're all blessed, or cursed. From Scarlett O'Hara and Rhett Butler, to Cathy and Heathcliff, to Darcy and Elizabeth Bennet, to Hercule Poirot ... we remember them all because their personalities were head and shoulders above the rest of the cast in their particular novels.

At another talk I gave (admittedly on short-story writing, but it's relevant here), a question was asked about names. I'm very keen on this subject, and the questioner was of the opposite opinion to me. Her argument was that it gave a short story an added air of mystery if you never named your characters at all. I saw her reasoning, but how often could you use the same ploy before it became tedious?

Obviously it wouldn't work in a novel and, to me, it would result in shadowy figures with no substance, because the first thing we do when we introduce people is to mention their names. Names are an extension of someone's personality, and while we're stuck with the ones our parents gave us, we can give our characters whatever names we choose. Many authors also do this by choosing pen-names to suit the style of their books, or for other reasons, including real-life anonymity.

More about names

Naming your characters should be as thought-provoking to you as naming your baby. They are both your creation, and just as you wouldn't give your baby any old tag, you should choose your fictional characters' names with care. In real life, you would firstly choose a first name that you liked, and also a name that went well with your surname. In fiction, writers so often forget to match these up, and

31

end up with some clumsy combination. Fine, if that's what you intended ...

And now it's confession time again. Morwen Tremayne married a Killigrew and then a Wainwright ... and Morwen Wainwright certainly isn't the easiest of names to say in your head, and even less so for the poor actress who eventually had to say it on audio cassette.

You see what I mean? I should have known better. But this can happen with a large cast of characters, even when you keep a running list of your characters' names beside you at all times when you're actually writing the novel, as I do. This helps to avoid having several characters with the same first names, and with too many names starting with the same initial, which can also be irritating. Do we really want to read about James, John, Jonathan and Jimmy all in the same chapter?

Even with all that, you can still overlook the practice of 'saying' the names in your head, as I did.

Choosing your characters' names – and considering the alternatives of established ones – can be a fascinating exercise. Would Billy Bloggins carry the same charisma as James Bond? The short, sharp combination sums up his quick-fire personality, and without any need for quirky names. Doesn't Ruth Rendell's Inspector Wexford conjure up the kind of man that he is? To me, it sounds solid and dependable, the epitome of a homely country copper despite his rank.

Matching characters to their locations and eras shouldn't cause you any problems. If you are writing about a Yorkshireman, you are unlikely to call him Wayne. Think nationally and regionally, and you will give your readers an instant impression of a man called Hamish MacNab, or a woman called Bronwen Jones. You *know* who they are.

The Guinness Book of Names by Leslie Dunkling will supply you with many interesting names and combinations, including the most popular boys' and girls' names during different decades and various regions of the world.

So, will it be plain or fancy or gimmicky? Whichever you choose can enhance your plot. John Mortimer's Rumpole is a marvellously named character. You can 'see' him without knowing a single thing about him. The same goes for one of his other characters, the elegantly named Claude Erskine-Brown. We hardly need to know that he is an 'opera-loving wine-buff'. The name says it all.

Play with names and see where they lead you, but don't forget that the reader will have certain expectations of your character because of what society has dictated. Again, Claude Erskine-Brown is a good example. We *expect* him to be snobbish and upper-class, or he'd have left the hyphen off his name long ago and reverted to being plain old Mr Brown.

It's doubtful whether the classic authors had any instruction in the way they wrote their novels. Which is perhaps why they defined their characters so cleverly and obviously by their choice of names. Consider the marvellously named characters in Thomas Hardy's *Far from the Madding Crowd*, and tell me if you could see them in any other way than the way he meant us to see them.

- Gabriel Oak – solid, dependable, strong, attractive, and clearly the right man for the heroine.
- Bathsheba – the use of long vowel sounds in this name makes it more romantic and slightly exotic.
- Sergeant Troy – efficient, sharp, a leader. Private

Troy wouldn't have sounded so earthy. Captain Troy would have been one step removed from romantic involvement.

- Fanny Robin – light, mischievous, good-time girl. The name is already a tease.
- Mr Boldwood – dull, older, set in his ways. The use of his full title gives him status, and removes him from any sense of familiarity.
- Soberness and Temperance Miller – your guess!

We undoubtedly 'see' people's names in certain ways. We don't react to an Elizabeth in the same way as Lizzie or Beth or Bess. We don't see Charles in the same light as Charlie or Chas or Chuck. Same name-route, different reaction. And be careful with dual-role names, such as Sam (Samuel/Samantha), not to confuse the reader before making things clear. Unless the *intention* is initially to confuse.

Character profiles

How much do you need to know about your characters before you begin, or should they just grow in your mind as your plot develops? Even though some authors will say this is the way they like to work, it can be a disastrous assumption for a beginner to make. All your characters must develop and mature during the course of your book, but they will still have a personal background, a life before the point at which the story began, and solid reasons for being in this book.

This is why I believe that creating a character profile of your central characters is as necessary as anything else you devise. Minor characters who don't need such in-depth information about them can be disregarded for the moment. But whether it's your romantic hero and heroine, your clever detective or your brilliant court coroner, give your characters life by creating a profile on them. In historical novels it's also useful to create an entire family tree of your intricate cast of characters.

If you find all this difficult to do, beyond a brief description of blue eyes and long dark hair and shapely figure; or the fact that Bergerac tore around the island of Jersey in that super car, whose name I can't now remember ... then think of someone you know well. As a test run, think of everything you know about him or her, and summarise it. The people we see every day are not normally detailed in our minds like this, because we have no need to memorise them. We simply know them.

For instance: my personal subject collects miniature china elephants. Still young, she's been married twice and has five children. She is petite and very strong-willed, a junior school governor and special needs assistant. She's intelligent and quick-witted and once worked as an accountant. She doesn't smoke or drink alcohol, but likes socialising with her many friends. Her team frequently wins quiz nights at the local pub. She plays golf, and usually wins at Scrabble.

She says she hates Christmas (until the last-minute frenzy), loves foreign holidays. Confides in friends far more than her family. Gets weepy over old films on TV, and can't watch anything medical or hurtful to children. Tough on the outside, but a softie at heart, and can be relied on to come to the rescue in any emergency.

And yes, she's my daughter. And I had to think really hard to put all that together, because, well, I just know her! This was only a brief sketch, but it is the kind of profile you should be writing for your main characters.

35

Filling in the gaps

There are many more things you could think of to add to your list. School backgrounds, tastes in music and books, colour preferences, jewellery, style of clothes, etc. Remember Inspector Morse and his love of opera? Such a simple detail marks him out as someone different from the run-of-the-mill fictional policeman. Susan Moody's feisty female detective, Cassie Swann, is a bridge professional. This again gives the character extra substance and reality – and the human touch.

No character should be 100 per cent perfect. How boring they would be if that were so. Super-brain Sherlock Holmes had his weaknesses, and was all the more human because of it. Scarlett O'Hara certainly had hers, and so did Heathcliff. Almost all of Hardy's characters were flawed in some way, and it didn't detract from their appeal to readers.

Give your characters virtues by all means, but give them faults as well. You don't have to go to extremes such as making them drug addicts or wife-beaters, but faults such as jealousy, a gambling tendency, a strong competitive streak or ruthlessness in business, impatience with lesser mortals – and spouses – will make them identifiable to many readers.

Remember that even while your plot may require your characters to do super-human things, your aim is to make them seem as human as possible to readers, and a permanent goody-two-shoes is more likely to be irritating than endearing.

And if you think all this character-profiling is time-wasting, Kieran Prendiville is reported as having created ten complete character profiles before he started on the plot of *Ballykissangel*.

A final tip. When you make your character pr write it out in the first person, as if *you* are Jane Doe. It will make her all the more real to you, because while you are describing her, you *are* her.

(I didn't do this in the example of my daughter's profile, since she is a real person.)

Goals and motivation

For the plot of a novel to have the forward movement it requires, your central characters need goals to reach, and the motivation to get there. Working out the goals you have in mind for your characters is also self-propelling, because it will help you to plan your story in a sequential manner.

The goal that your main character will eventually attain will depend largely on his motivation and nature, but also on the obstacles that life and other characters produce to prevent any easy route. So when you create each character profile, remember that their talents, faults, goals and motivation are an aid to plotting.

If you write a story about a wimp, then to keep him in character, his actions will be wimpish, the story is likely to be slower-paced to the point of tedium, and his motivation will probably be nil. If you write about a tough bounty-hunter, then, by definition, the story will be stronger, tenser, and his/her motivation will be ready-made and much stronger, and open the way to dramatic situations.

Ask yourself the following questions.

- Have you created a strong enough central character to carry the story through?
- Does he (she) have the necessary intelligence to

know what he wants and to go all out to get it?

- Has he the gumption to withstand outside pressures that threaten to thwart these goals?
- Will he survive against all the odds?
- Is he quick-witted, literate, adaptable to the plot changes you have detailed for him?
- Do you like him and therefore are sympathetic to all that you're asking him to do in the plot?
- And have you understood him so well that if he walked into a room, you would instantly know him, and what makes him tick? You should.

Emotional involvement

Everyone knows the old adage 'Make 'em laugh, make 'em cry, make 'em wait'. It's intended for a theatre audience, of course, but you can apply the same kind of quote to any fictional medium.

What it really means is that you should give your characters as much emotional involvement in the plot as you can. It's no use writing about a character who is suffering intense guilt because he hasn't reported a road accident in which he was involved, unless you describe how he is *feeling*. The author who metaphorically stands on the sidelines and merely says the character doesn't know what to do at that traumatic moment, and so on, is copping out.

It's what is known in the writing game as Telling, not Showing. You have probably heard this phrase, maybe more positively, as 'Show, don't Tell'. Simply, it means involving your characters in all the scenes in your book, from the big vast actions covering a huge canvas, such as a battle scene or violent murder, to the desperately

38

emotional feelings of a woman on hearing that her husband has been killed on some military mission in a far-off country.

Appealing to all the senses is one of the most astute ways of bringing your characters to life. Just as we feel and experience life through our senses, so should they – and they should be shown to do so.

Lovers of all ages will respond to hearing a favourite, haunting song reminding them of some special time spent together – and they will frequently echo the sentiments they may be unable to express in words. A special scent, even of something as simple as pine needles, or roses, or new-mown hay, will evoke nostalgic memories. Alternatively, the smell of a dead tramp who has lain in his own filth for days will evoke disgust – but you'll register it!

The sight of a sleeping baby in a pram can be heart-breaking to a woman who has had her own child stolen or taken from her by authority. The taste of certain foods can be evocative, as can the taste of a cool drink sliding down the throat on a blazingly hot day. The taste of a lover's skin can be extremely sensual. The more intangible but very real taste of fear can come from the thought of speaking in public or facing a first interview; to being held up at gun-point or caught shop-lifting; or taking a first flight in a balloon.

How about touch? This must surely be the most useful sense of all for an author to exploit. Some examples: the touch of velvet; of cat's fur; of bird's feathers; of snow; of warm flesh; of the cold steel of a gun; of feeling a hot spurt of blood from a knife-wound.

In letting your characters use all these senses, you are also reaching your readers' senses and getting an emotional reaction from them. And, believe me, this is what keeps them reading, and this is what you should be aiming for.

Always remember that if your plot is character-driven, which, I repeat, is what I think is the essence of every plot, then those characters must live their lives to the full. This means letting them have the capability to experience all that real life would offer them. Depending on your book, they may not go through the range of every emotion, but you and your readers should believe that they could cope with exhilaration or disaster, or whatever else, if required to do so. They may not always cope *well,* but they would face up to it.

Viewpoint

Are you going to write your book from the first-person viewpoint, or in the more usual third-person? This is not only a matter of personal choice, but can be dependent on the kind of book you write, and the publisher you are aiming for. In the latter case, the publisher most likely to refuse a first person novel is Harlequin Mills & Boon, but if you planned a novel for them, you would do your homework by reading a number of their books, and sending for guidelines, etc.

It's more difficult to sustain a book in the first person, because everything that happens in it must be seen, heard and experienced through that central 'I' character.

There is a limit as to the number of times 'I' can look in a mirror and see how 'I' appear. There are ways of getting around this in dialogue with another person, of course, by letting them comment on how ill/pale/excited/attractive 'I' look, but this style of writing has many limitations.

I have only written three novels using the first-person

narrative. Two were Gothic novels, in which first-person narratives are very effective. One of these was told from a young man's viewpoint, the other from the heroine's viewpoint. The Gothic novel always involves an eerie old house or castle, and a mysterious atmosphere. It is often set in locations such as deepest Yorkshire or mysterious Scotland or Cornwall. The heroine is always in deadly danger. There are often two men involved, and the reader is never quite sure which one is the hero or which the villain. Lovely to write, but not quite so much favoured nowadays.

My other first-person narrative was a teenage novel from a boy's viewpoint. These were three of my early novels, following my experience with writing magazine 'confession' stories – also essentially first-person narratives. This type of narrative has its supporters, but I think there is more scope for publication in the third-person narrative.

NB: In long sagas, using more than one (third-person) viewpoint can be used very successfully, illustrating the activities of several main characters. The bonus effect of using multi-viewpoints in this way is in moving the plot along at a changing pace and at different levels, in exactly the same way as television soap operas do.

In fictional terms, you are jolting the reader and keeping the interest alive by applying lateral thinking. For example, Chapter 1 may end on a dramatic note with one central character, then Chapter 2 might begin with another, leaving the outcome of Chapter 1 temporarily suspended. To do this well, you must ensure that the threads of the plot are linked. This is certainly a case where plotting in detail has great advantage over a rambling affair.

Importance of dialogue

Imagine yourself being introduced to someone at a party. Do you stand like a dummy and say nowt? I think not. What do you think the reaction of the other person would be? Either he'd think you were boring, or an idiot, or too star-struck to speak, depending on his status to your own. Unless he felt you were genuinely ill (in which case why aren't you home in bed?), he'd soon get fed up with this one-sided affair, and turn to someone who was more interesting and responsive.

Dialogue between the characters is an essential part of any novel. Dialogue is also a two-way thing, and does more for your plot than just varying the look of the prose with those speech marks. By letting the characters talk to one another, they learn something about each other. It is also a painless and revealing way of letting the reader in on whatever you want them to know.

Imagine for a moment that your fictional criminals are planning a big art robbery. You could describe the outline of the plan in a single page of prose ... but how much more effective it would be to get in on the act in the old warehouse where they habitually meet, to let them discuss and argue and discard their ideas while trying to time their scam down to the minutest detail.

By letting the characters 'speak' to one another in this situation, you can indicate to the readers which are the strongest characters, and where the weak link lies. Don't ever underestimate the power of dialogue between your characters in moving your story forward by suggestion and implication.

There's no doubt that some writers find dialogue terribly difficult to write. I always advise people to try to 'hear' their characters speaking their lines. Listen to them in your head or, if you prefer it, speak them out loud, or into a tape-recorder. Practise the dialogue on your nearest and dearest if you can bear to, and see what response you get. Or ask a sympathetic other to take one of the parts for you, and act out the scenes as if they are in a play.

Use whatever method you like as long as it results in dialogue that is right for those characters. And always, always give each one a voice that is his own. None of your characters should speak in such interchangeable voices that the reader isn't sure who's who.

No Yorkshireman would speak in a West Country accent, as I do, so while you are writing his dialogue, forget your own voice and think in terms of your character's. If your man is a Yorkshire Dales farmer, then 'rehearse' his lines, outwardly or inwardly, in a Yorkshire accent. Who knows, you may end up as a budding actor on the side ...

Visualisation

Many writers say they have difficulty in 'seeing' their characters. They can describe them on paper, but they still can't really imagine what they look like. If this is your problem, you could try to find a magazine picture of someone who approximates your character's outward appearance.

Or maybe you have unconsciously based your character on someone you admire (or not) in the media or in films. In other words, used a role model.

By actively having a photo of that person in front of you as you write, you may be able to portray your fictional character more accurately. Unless you are foolish enough to call your character by a media person's name, or plot your novel with his particular virtues or misdemeanours as part of the main action, it's highly unlikely that any reader would associate the fiction with the fact.

Summary

- Good characters are the pivot of any novel.
- Get to know your characters by profiling them.
- Enhance their personalities by the choice of names.
- Always give them motivation and goals.
- Give each one an individual voice.
- Use role models to define characters.

4

SYNOPSIS AND PLOT – CREATIVE PARTNERS

Whenever I want to read a book, I write one
Benjamin Disraeli

How do you actually write a synopsis, and what's the difference between that and the plot? I've lost count of the times that question has been asked during a lecture or writing course. They *are* creative partners, but there's no hard and fast rule that says you need the one to produce the other. Or even in which order you write them.

Many writers like or need both. Others need only the bare bones of the synopsis as a kind of prop to push them from the beginning to the end of the novel. Others need the full-blown, detailed plot as guidance. And the lucky few start to write quite happily with a sentence or two and let the book lead where it will. (The latter approach can be tricky for beginners though, especially if you have the kind of rambling mind that wanders away from the central storyline.)

So does a beginner writer need a brief synopsis first or a complex plot outline? Since we are all individuals, it really all depends on you; on your imagination; on your skill and confidence at controlling your thoughts and keeping them in some kind of order; and ... well, maybe now you see why some folk prefer to know where they're going by having the safety-net of some pre-arranged plan for the book.

One thing is for sure. Whether you have a sketchy

synopsis or a detailed plot at your side to guide you, you will be avoiding the dreaded writer's block – and the thought of staring at a blank page or screen without a shred of inspiration. And it doesn't take away the spontaneity of the writing process, because you haven't started the book yet. When you actually begin Chapter 1, this is where the real sparkle comes in. So away with any doubts on that score.

Which comes first? And what is the difference?

Assuming that you are going to write both, then it really doesn't matter whether or not you write the synopsis first and then build on it to create your plot. Or whether you plan out your plot in rambling detail, refine it and sharpen it, and then condense it into a synopsis for possible editorial submission, or merely for your own quick reference.

There are no hard and fast rules, so don't be deluded into thinking that you won't produce a saleable book if you don't stick to rigid guidelines, because I'm not giving you any. Many writers work out the plot first of all, which can sometimes seem like a great haphazard muddle, throwing in everything that could be of use in the story, and then cutting it into a sharper synopsis. This is often my way.

But wait a moment. Because there is a difference in the synopsis you may end up with for your own guidance, and the more professional one that you submit to an editor. Your own sketchy one-liners, if that's how your personal synopsis results, can sit happily by your side as you write the book, while the one that you send to an editor must be far more professional. But both can be used as a quick reference to keep you on the central path of your plot, without the detail of filling in scenes and the necessary extra characters who will almost certainly appear as you flesh out your story.

Creating your synopsis

Let's assume that you are going to work on the synopsis first, if only because you don't have to do the hard work of putting in too much detail at this stage. Let's also assume that this is the synopsis you are going to offer to a publisher, with or without the first three chapters of your book.

NB: A synopsis will enable an editor to see the shape of your proposed novel, but without the first few chapters he can have no idea of your writing style. It's rare for a publisher to commission a novel on the basis of a synopsis alone, unless you are already an established author and he knows your work. At that stage you may readily get the novel commissioned on the basis of the synopsis.

So where do you begin? First, the editor needs to know the period in which you are setting your book, and the names of the characters who are going to appear in it. He needs to know the type of book this will be, i.e. thriller, romance, science fiction, etc. There is absolutely no future in keeping an editor in suspense while you write some whimsical piece in order to keep him guessing and 'intrigue' him. It won't. It will only annoy him.

Some people will state the above requirements in a small box or short paragraph at the beginning. Personally I simply give the run-down of the story. Others will include samples of dialogue. I do not, and nor do I think it's necessary at this stage, since it simply holds up the flow of the synopsis, which is also the essence or the core of the plot.

The synopsis should be a précis of the entire novel without fleshing out individual scenes. It should be brief enough not to wander off the track, but still prove to the editor that there is enough substance and texture in it to produce a novel. Remember *shape*. The editor needs to know the shape of the novel, and that it has a sharp beginning, a sustaining middle section, and a resolutory ending.

Dialogue and writing style can be more effectively shown in the first three chapters that you would normally offer with the synopsis.

NB: Always send the *first three chapters*, not random ones selected throughout the book. This will definitely not impress the editor.

What is more important at this stage is to assure the editor that you know how to construct a novel, and that you have created sufficiently strong characters to carry that story through. Always ask yourself if your story is really going anywhere, and prove it by constructing a solid story-line that takes your characters safely to their required conclusion. Getting there is basically all that a synopsis does. And once an editor takes an interest in your proposed story, he will often suggest changes at this initial stage.

The astute author will be prepared to adapt and compromise to a degree, although I don't believe you should be browbeaten into changing *everything* on the whim of an editor. But remember that he is the one who is going to buy your book, hopefully, and pay you money for it, and nothing is more certain to annoy an editor who knows his business than a precious would-be author who doesn't.

Backgrounds and settings

The background of your novel can have an enormous influence on how you are going to plan it. Locations can dictate how your characters will react and behave. A pretty English village may suggest a quiet, pastoral scene with a gentle plot, but may well hide seething passions among its characters, and has been a favourite background for crime writers.

The following settings all suggest different types of characters and different life-styles, and can determine the pace of your novel.

- Manor houses in creepy backwaters.
- Country estates with vast acreages.
- Castles in Spain.
- Mysterious gothic Scotland.
- Cornish mining.
- Industrial northern mining towns.

If you choose to write about such backgrounds and settings, think about the kind of people who would live or work there. The very rich may be indolent or selfish or perfectly charming – and innocent to the point of being victimised by their own charm. Workers in the same setting may be jealous to the point of rage and murderous thoughts. All give scope for plotting.

Backgrounds and settings have played a major part in plotting my own novels, which is why I always describe myself as a 'background first' writer. The background for my novels has always helped me to decide on the characters and their journey through my book.

I want to reiterate a specific point here. I don't mean to imply that trying to fit characters into a preconceived plot would work. It might, but it would be a very contrived premise. But I do pre-plan where the characters live, the era in which they live, their social backgrounds, and any historical or national or international events in which they might become involved. This is merely the *background* to my story, and all of it together leads me to finding my characters and developing my plot.

Characters living and working in an historical novel set in the Australian Outback, for instance, would have vastly different behaviour patterns and pace of life from those living and working in a contemporary, glittering Las Vegas casino. I have used both backgrounds, and the influences of these choices on any creative writer should be obvious.

The former might face hardship, dust storms, dangers and deprivations; the latter would lead a far more glamorous life, involved in show-biz, perhaps, or with Mafia undertones ... in my way of working, no plot would be involved in my thinking yet, but the kind of characters inhabiting such settings would be stirring in my mind.

As a mental exercise, take a few moments to think of a city such as Amsterdam. Even if you only have a smattering of knowledge about the place, a number of interesting facts might come to your mind.

- Diamonds.
- Drugs.
- The Red-Light district.
- Canals.
- Cheese-making.
- Clog-making.
- Flower markets.
- KLM International airport.

You haven't begun to do any real research yet, but those various facts alone could start an imaginative author's mind working on finding certain types of characters and the beginnings of a plot. That's the way my mind works, and it has always produced successful results.

As indicated already, locations are not the only useful backgrounds you can find. Specific events can trigger ideas that can produce plots. Every battle you can think of can be the source of a novel, whether you encompass the entire Second World War in your story, or choose an important event such as D-Day, the General Strike, the Great Exhibition of 1851, anniversaries, regional or international. These could all be utilised as a starting-point for your plot.

There are also completely imaginary settings. They may be based on actual locations, or not. One of my American historical sagas was loosely based on the island of Crete, but it had its own name and villages, and was created entirely out of my imagination. It's a cringe-making cliché, but the world is truly your oyster when it comes to backgrounds for your plots – and every one can produce a pearl ...

The all-important What If factor

The writer who doesn't constantly ask questions about where the story is going, or if the characters would logically do and say what you are asking them to, is only doing half a job. The choices the author makes are what make each story different from the next one.

One of the questions I have sometimes been asked is how I make all my books different, or do I simply regurgitate the early ones! I certainly hope I don't do that, and nor is there any need to do so. Every one of us is unique, and every character you create should be just as unique. Each one of them has come out of your imagination, and nobody knows them as well as you do. They will interact with other unique characters of your creation, and in turn, each set of characters will be involved in different problems, goals, life-styles and backgrounds.

This is how every book becomes different, and the so-called 'formula' writing so looked down upon in romantic novels mostly comes from people who never read them. Do they sneer at *Jane Eyre*, or *Pride and Prejudice*, or *Tess of the D'Urbervilles*? Romantic novels all, whatever the purists might say. There's no compulsion to read anything you don't like, but all credit should be given to romantic authors for their ingenuity and skill in writing the novels that millions of readers buy.

Few authors would want their books to be clones of those that have gone before, whether their own work, or by plagiarising others. The only true formula that is followed in every book in every genre is that it has to have a beginning, a middle and an end.

But you may begin to suspect that you *are* plotting a story that sounds vaguely familiar, however unintentionally. You may even be asking your characters to follow a certain path that has gone before. If that happens, stop and ask yourself the most important question that any novelist can ask of himself. This is the *What If* question.

For instance, what if your character had a change of heart and did completely the opposite to what the reader is expecting? Runs out on the bridegroom at the altar, perhaps? Yes, it's been done before, but it's still the opposite of what the reader would logically expect to happen.

NB: Although a change of heart may be logical in the character's mind at the time, there's also a case for it to be *completely illogical*. Don't we all do crazy things on the spur of the moment, however regrettable it might turn out to be? Let your characters surprise your readers sometimes, providing that you have worked out their reasons in your own mind, for what they do. This is where your detailed character profile is invaluable, because you *know* why she would be behaving temporarily out of character.

Making choices is a great part of the plotting process. What if the big dramatic scene you envisage never takes place at all? Can you really afford to tease the reader in this way, and still provide a feasible twist in the plot? I have done this on more than one occasion, but it *must* be done with forethought, and not thrown in as a diversion. Let me explain how I used this device.

It came in a Harlequin Mills & Boon historical that I always refer to as my *Titanic* novel. As always, with my 'background first' plotting, I had always wanted to write a *Titanic* novel ... and it was written long before the movie came out... In my book, *A Gentleman's Masquerade* (writing as Sally Blake), my central character had booked her passage to America on the *Titanic,* and a good part of the book led up to this event. I had several choices here.

Everyone knows the *Titanic* story, so if I was going to let my heroine be drowned, her part in the book would have ended. I'll leave you to work out for yourself if I chose this option. If she survived, what became of her from then on? Was this how I wanted to develop the book? And what effect would it have on her if I took this option?

Or what if she didn't travel at all? And if she didn't, what sensible reason could there be for her giving up the voyage of a lifetime? Would she be traumatised by thinking about the unknown person who had bought her ticket? Or want to find out who he was, and make compensation to his/her family? These and many other questions had to be answered ...

It is always a fascinating experience to work on the What If theory, and to keep it in mind while you are devising your plot. Writing is a creative medium, and how you decide on your characters' motivations and develop your plot accordingly is one of the things that makes your book unique to you.

A plot is a sequence of events that involve your characters, pushing them forward to the end of your novel. It can be likened to a chain, where every link must be joined in some way to the events that have gone before, and are going to influence the ones that come next.

But while you are still puzzling over how to get from A to Z, never be afraid to discard anything that doesn't feel right to you at this stage. Until you actually submit your work to an editor, everything that you write can be pushed to the back of a drawer, ripped to shreds, or committed to the waste-paper basket. Not that I honestly recommend any of those things. It hurts! And it can always be improved.

So be prepared to work on your book until it is the very best that you can make it. If that means plotting and re-plotting until you get it right, then the day an editor offers you a contract, you'll know it was worth all the effort.

Using flashbacks

There is no doubt that the word 'flashback' bothers a

great many people. In its simplest term, all it means is that you are giving the readers some information about events that have happened before your story began.

The most tedious, and least recommended way to do this is to spend a couple of chapters filling in the information before you get to the 'here and now' of the story. This is comparable to treading water. Filtering in that information, through dialogue and short scenes, is the more subtle way, and one that doesn't hold up the forward movement of your plot.

There will be many times in your book when you need to refer to something that has gone before. Characters do not live in a vacuum, and they have had past lives before your story began. These lives may have no *immediate* bearing on the way your plot develops, in which case it may not be necessary to do more than bring in short pieces of information from time to time. But everything we have done in the past shapes our lives, including the people we have met, our families, colleagues, and the events, good or bad, that we have experienced. There are very few novels that exist without *some* reference to past events in the characters' lives, and they will have more substance in being shown as complete people.

Supposing your main character has some hang-up about hospitals, and severe bouts of depression. The reader needs to know why. You can't just drop in this phobia without some explanation, maybe about witnessing a previous horrendous traffic accident, or a more personal hospital experience. It would certainly warrant a flashback scene of some kind, and this would in turn create reader-sympathy for the character.

To give an example of how a flashback can further the plotting process, consider as a character a 38-year-old ambitious, feminist politician. She did not arrive at that elevated position in her life like Aphrodite springing ready-formed out of the sea.

Such a character screams out for providing the reader with some background information. Of course she (the character) may be a wonderful person who has gone serenely from university into politics with the ease of slipping into a pair of comfortable shoes, and with no problems in her past life at all. Such admirable, but fictionally mundane experiences wouldn't make an interesting or page-turning book. So look at her with a more critical eye.

Was she always so single-minded? Was there some scandal in her life, or some secret that she has successfully hidden all these years? And is there someone else lurking in the background, all too ready to uncover it? Does this not smack of ransoms, blackmail, illegitimate children, drug-handling, kiss-and-tell newspaper disclosures?

I am not here to offer ready-made plots, and nor am I suggesting that you would throw all those things at this poor unfortunate woman. But there are some situations that simply present themselves to an imaginative author as the basis for a good meaty plot, and this is certainly one of them.

Past information about characters has to be given to the reader in some way, often by the use of flashback. Using the above scenario as an example, there are various ways in how it could be done. The information can be revealed through the character's own thoughts, maybe included as a chunk of information as she reflects on how successful she has become, despite her earlier misdemeanours. And maybe she's still counting her lucky chances, and wondering if her luck will eventually run out.

The flashback can occur by reading a snippet in a

newspaper referring to someone in her past. Is he about to rake up names and so on, for the sensational scandal-rag, and would she, or should she contact him to stop him at all costs? The ideas from this one scenario alone are endless.

The flashback could come through letters, as he demands money to keep his mouth shut. The correspondent then would be providing some or all of the flashback information, perhaps enclosing photographs, and enabling the character to consider what she is seeing and reading and in doing so revealing more of the background to the reader. How she dealt with all of this would further the plot.

Actually, I rather like this one myself. And it all comes out of asking questions, because when you ask yourself questions, you automatically supply some of the answers. They may not be the right answers first time out but, with luck, you will get there in the end.

Prologues and epilogues

Flashbacks, prologues and epilogues are all ways of giving the reader information. A prologue can be a neat and concise way of doing this at the beginning of a novel. It can be a brief one-page affair, or it can be virtually a short chapter in its own right. I used this longer method in one of my books, *Willow Harvest* (writing as Rowena Summers). The prologue told a brief history of the mysterious Somerset area where my book was set, where the countryfolk were suspicious of strangers. It included some brief but telling dialogue – in every sense.

Through the dialogue between several old country characters, it brought in the old legends of the area, and referred briefly to the newcomers who bore the same name as some previously hanged characters. Suspicion, mystery and village closed-ranks characters were hinted at very early on.

The real story began with Chapter 1, with the heroine and her family arriving in a new community. By using the prologue as a teaser, the reader already knew there was conflict to come, and it didn't hold up any of the action.

It's also a useful device, particularly in an historical novel, to state the year at the beginning of the prologue and again at the beginning of the first chapter, if necessary, especially if time has moved on.

An epilogue is something that comes at the end of a novel, and winds everything up neatly. It is not so commonly used nowadays as it used to be, but if it is used, it should be brief. It can be at its most effective when you want to push the story a little further forward in time.

You might want to state that your romantic characters returned to the place they met and eventually married on a certain date, for instance. Or, while the real hero in your story is the hick American private eye who got his man, you may want to add a rider that the convicted criminal in your thriller finally got his just deserts and was sent to the electric chair ...

NB: Remember to check that the American State where you set this thriller still uses the electric chair as its death penalty. Or did so at the time your book was set.

It may happen that you feel you really do need to add these riders, but that they don't fit in with the style of the previous writing. So it feels more comfortable to simply state the facts in a small detail at the end as an epilogue. But as I said, it's not used so much nowadays, and I wouldn't recommend it as an easy way to finish off what should be resolved through your characters and the events of your plot.

There is one more way of supplying previous information in a technique that I have only seen once. The first half page of each chapter was written in italics, covering the relevant flashback detail. The rest of each chapter then continued with the normal plot progression. It may be too quirky a way of working to appeal to many publishers – or authors – but in the book concerned it was very effective.

Summary

- Write synopsis or plot in the order that suits you.
- Choice of backgrounds can trigger your plot.
- Always ask yourself questions – especially What If?
- Keep flashbacks under control.

5

THINKING LOGICALLY

There are certain things a writer needs before he can start
writing ... like a story
Rodney Trotter – Only Fools and Horses

Rambling is a great pastime for those who enjoy fresh
air and getting out into the countryside, but rambling is
no way to write a saleable book. The most successful
authors know where they're going. The author Julian
Rathbone puts it even more strongly. He says he
distrusts authors who say they don't know how a book
will evolve when they begin, and that the characters
'take on a life of their own'.

Of course, the characters *do* have lives of their own,
because your book is all about them and not you, but
never lose sight of the fact that they are the lives that you
have created for them. You can make them do anything
you want them to do, but you must always be in control
of them, or your book may well waffle off into the realms
of nowhere.

Others will disagree, but since this book is about
plotting your novel, and *I* am in control of it! (mostly ...),
then the way you put the plot together will show whether
or not you have the wherewithal for solid construction, or
if you are ending up with a house of straw.

It comes back to question-time again. Questioning
your characters and the things you are expecting them to
do will do more to sort out the logical events from the
impossible or downright ridiculous than anything else, yet

many beginners overlook it.

Question yourself in this context too, and ask if you are tackling something that is beyond you. Fantasy is one thing, but once your readers start to disbelieve anything that you give your characters to do, you've lost them. And as well as basic character traits that come into play with these questions, take a good hard look at the overall shape of your plot and be sure that it all hangs together.

Suspending disbelief always seems an odd phrase to me, but it's what all authors do when they write their novels. In effect, we are inviting readers into an entirely imaginary world of our own making, asking them to share it, and persuading – and expecting – them to believe that it's real. To do that, we must first persuade ourselves that it's real.

So, consider a few of the questions you might ask when you take that overall look at your initial planning. Naturally, these will depend on the kind of book you are writing, and it's not a wasted task to work out a list of them for your own adaptation. For instance:

- Have you developed a logical way for your adventurous hero to behave, so that his daring deeds don't descend into the world of farce and incredibility?
- Would your gentle heroine really ask her lover to break into a bank, or wreck her stalker's car? Readers would never take this without intelligent characterisation.
- Would your sensible woman teacher reasonably throw up her safe steady job to sail around the world, simply as an act of rebellion? *Give her good reasons, and she might!*
- Would your six-year-old character really use such

a vast vocabulary, and react to bullying in the cool adult manner you describe? (Listen to six-year-olds in school playgrounds – just take care not to appear as another kind of stalker. There is danger in all things ...)

If the answers to any of those basic questions is *Yes,* and you have logically worked out that it could happen, and that your readers would be cheering him or her on ... *Then, go for it*!

But if the answers are *No,* or *Doubtful,* then think again. Readers are keen-eyed when it comes to spotting an impossible or unlikely situation, and your crucial first reader will be an agent or an editor who has read it all before ...

Methodical construction

There is nothing quite so satisfying as reaching the end of your detailed plot, reviewing it with a critical eye, and realising that you have a workable and logically constructed story to tell. At first, creating that plot out of thin air may seem like an uphill task, but if you are writing a novel based on something you feel passionate about, it doesn't come solely out of thin air at all.

Does that surprise you? It shouldn't. I've already said that a great deal of the planning takes place in the head and the subconscious. To the beginner author this may seem like a wild assumption, but we all dream of some goal we'd like to attain. Winning the lottery, perhaps – and what you would do if it ever happened to you.

My husband says the first thing we would do is hop on the first plane to somewhere and get away from everyone until the fuss had died down. That's *his* dream, and it usually extends to how we would go (Concorde), where we would go (around the world), what we would buy (Rolls-Royce for him, maybe a yacht. Don't know for me – possibly a publishing house!), etc.

This has all the makings of a plot, however brief and scatty and unresolved and unlikely, coming straight out of the imagination, from a practical man who isn't a writer and has no ambitions to be. Dare I say 'Thank God'!

We all have the potential to be dreamers, to use our subconscious, and to let various ideas roam around in our heads. It's the best way I know of marshalling the events into a story-line, eventually arriving at a workable plot.

Before I begin serious plotting, I spend time dreaming of everything that could go into my potential novel, and jotting down all I can think of to flesh out the story. These are still 'plot thoughts'. The embryo novel does not yet have a fully formed plot, nor even a synopsis, but these ideas, suggestions, dreams, etc., tell me what I think could go into my novel. I'm not only using my imagination, but digging deep into my mind for what I want to put into my book and, most importantly, the path my characters are going to take.

I probably revise these ideas more times than I do the eventual novel itself. By the time I come to write it I have sorted out the jumble and worked out what needs to be said in a methodical way, which includes discarding extraneous characters and scenes that add nothing to the story. But the methodical construction that I hopefully end up with doesn't happen by accident.

It's a bit like moving house. After the initial horror of finding unnumbered packing cases and the hopeless task of ever getting the rooms straight and deciding you really don't need half of it any more, and you didn't really want to move anyway, you finally start to get your house in order. Even then, you can still find bits of junk you don't want, or find something you had forgotten, and give it pride of place.

Don't ever be so inflexible over your plot that you can't allow these gems to shine through and liven up a scene or a chapter. It happens, and the more you write, the more you realise it. Who said 'There's more in heaven and earth than we ever dream of?' Probably no-one in *exactly* those words. But that just proves my point. Because nobody says it quite like you do, or quite like I do. *It* being your book – and mine.

Too much, too soon

In constructing your plot, try to pace it without artificially forcing that pace. This may sound odd, but when you begin to write the novel itself, there is often a great temptation to throw everything at the reader in the first few pages. And why not, since you will have been told to draw the reader quickly into the world you have created? This is all true.

But that comes with the actual writing, when your sparkling characterisation and dramatic background detail will intrigue readers and encourage them to read on. It is not throwing the entire plot at them in the first few pages. Think about it. If they learn everything there is to know by page 10, why bother to read any more? You will have run out of steam, and the plot will be going downhill from then on.

Writing and re-writing the plot outline gives you a chance to know how much you want to say at the beginning, and how to hold back on important twists in the story.

Keep them guessing

The crime novel that produces a corpse on page 1 will only be effective if the author keeps readers guessing until the end, as the police or amateur detectives sort out the various suspects and discard them. The writer will have his murderer's identity well planned and disguised, but his skill in keeping the readers guessing is what keeps them turning the pages.

The balancing act

Stumbling upon my old 'numbers method' of plotting, which I referred to earlier on, taught me the value of pacing. In my 20 potential chapters, I literally spaced out the high peaks and the lower troughs, for want of a better expression. Few novels can exist on a perpetual 'high'. You need to provide calmer episodes among the dramatic events, if only to give those more impact and to make more scenic contrasts – and also to give readers time to draw breath.

The novel that plods along without these variations would be dull indeed. Tease the readers about what's going to come later, because that will keep them reading. But don't put all your scintillating plotting into the first half of the book, then drift on towards the end like a boat without a rudder. If you do that, you've only got half a book. The rest is padding.

Once you get into the habit of pacing your novel's events, you automatically balance it. Put yourself in a reader's shoes. Isn't it extremely irritating to read a book where all the action happens at the beginning? The essence of a good book is for the reader to constantly wonder what is going to happen next. He may not consciously be doing this, but that's what novels are all about. Telling stories.

Something must always be 'going to happen next' in a novel, or you have no story to tell. Your characters will be getting into all kinds of situations, whether they are dramatic or adventurous, horrific or domestic. In doing so, they will be experiencing the whole range of emotional hang-ups, conflicts and difficulties, from which you have to logically extract them, by seemingly allowing *them* to solve everything by their own efforts.

Young children get it right when they write their first stories, and almost every sentence begins with the words 'And then ... And then ... And then ...' Out of the mouths and pencils of babes, and all that, comes something we could all learn. Their stories are inevitably very short, but if you ever get the chance to read one of them, you will find that they think in a delightfully sequential way, which could be because they haven't yet learned the deviousness of adults!

Children still have the clarity of thinking that's essential to good story-writing. But between the covers of a novel that may contain anything from fifty thousand to a quarter of a million words, you need twists and turns to sustain the events throughout the plot. In doing so, you will also control it.

Jigsaw puzzles and building blocks

Plotting a novel can be likened to doing a jigsaw puzzle. You have all those disjointed pieces to play around with that must fit together smoothly without forcing, and in the end presents you with a beautiful picture. Trying to make the pieces fit can seem like a nightmare to begin with but, as in any jigsaw, the pieces that don't go together will jar on you.

Another analogy that I always think applies very well to successful plotting is that of children's building blocks. If you think of these in pyramid form, and have ever watched the children master it, they build from the base up. There is a solid foundation of, say, a dozen blocks, with a smaller number in each layer as the pyramid grow towards its peak. It's necessary to keep the construction more and more finely balanced, until you reach that peak, which, in fictional terms, is the summit of all your efforts. The pyramid shape is sharpening your plotting all the way to its resolution.

Those dozen building blocks in the beginning represent your characters, their problems, their possible choices, the red herrings you will throw at them and so on. As you start to build, these possibilities will diminish, but the focus on the end result will be that much sharper. There will be fewer and fewer blocks left before you reach your stunning final piece, which is when you will metaphorically reach those magical two words that is the goal of every novelist: The End.

Any tutor can go on endlessly with analogies and comparisons, and hopefully they will all make sense. Take note of whichever one suits you best. But what you really want to know is how to construct and control that elusive mass of thoughts and turn them into a saleable plot.

Is your plot really adequate for its length?

But first of all I want to come back to that perennial worry for beginners: the length of the novel. If they are not concerned about it, they should be, and those that are, are also frequently embarrassed to ask about it in public.

Let's face it, when you're in an audience of wannabe writers listening to an eminent writer speak, you can feel very inhibited about asking some basic question. You always think everyone else knows the answer, anyway. Just remember that everyone else may be just as reticent as you for speaking up, but enquiring about length is not a question to be dismissed or scoffed at by more experienced writers.

You must be sure you have enough material in your planned story for the length you intend it to be. You know that. But what length *is* it? This is something you certainly need to get right, because the way you plan and plot will very much depend on it. Publishers also have a great deal to say about the subject, and for good reasons.

Genre novels conform very much in this way. Harlequin Mills & Boon romance novels require certain lengths – send for their guidelines – and there are more outlets in that one publishing house alone than the contemporary romance of 55,000 words. Their historical, for instance, require between 75,000 and 85,000 words. Your historical romance would be rejected out of hand if it was considerably shorter or twice as long. Market research is something no fiction writer should forget.

Crime novels and so-called 'straight' fiction are not usually as long as sagas or mainstream novels, but I stress that this is only a general rule. Each publisher will have his own ideas on the length of their books. Writing for guidelines is useful, but not all publishers supply them.

The simplest way of all to determine the length of the kind of book you want to write, is to read what's on the bookshelves. Instant research is there for the taking, and if a published book is 200 or 500 pages long, you will at least get a fair idea of the amount of plotting that it needs without the tedious task of counting every word.

Whatever the length of your proposed novel turns out to be, be sure you have enough of a plot to warrant that amount of writing. You can only gauge this by using your imagination and your research into your theme and your characters. It's far better to start out with too much detail, and be prepared to cut it down, than to try to stretch out a thin plot. All successful authors are prepared to prune their work, if only because, as authors, we know we are wordy people.

Most beginners overestimate the length that their books will be, if only because we are wordy people. But let's face it, if we didn't enjoy the physical shape and the aesthetic sense of words, we wouldn't be in the business that we are.

Pruning your work to make it as good as you can get it doesn't mean being ruthless with every sentence just because somebody told you to do so. Oh boy, is this my hobby-horse! I strongly believe that there's a great danger of revising so hard that you're left without any of the emotion and fully realised characterisation that you started out with.

Nor do I agree with the lofty quote that you should look for your best bits of writing, and cut them out. Personally, I think that is a ludicrous statement, since your best bits are surely those that you've worked on hardest to perfect.

I interpret this statement as meaning that you should cut out any 'precious' writing, including the kind of elaborate (and lengthy) paragraphs that are over-pompous. The kind that try very hard to impress on the reader that you are more educated / better informed / have a finer grasp of language / and that you know far longer words and clever-clever phrases than anybody else.

And another thing ... the notion that you should 'cut out your best bits' is attributed to Samuel Johnson, whose life-span was 1700–84. Would that all our comments were still being taken seriously after three hundred years – but with adaptation to the times, methinks!

The plotting graph

There are more ways than one of plotting a novel, and by now you will know that it is as individual as breathing. If the pyramid effect doesn't appeal to you, then when you are working out your plan of action, try to think of it as a graph. The plot may begin to move quite slowly at the bottom of the graph, gradually reaching small peaks and troughs, but always moving upwards towards a climax.

If you think of your novel in this way (perhaps using the 1 to 20 numbers method as a temporary guide for the moment), then before the end of your novel there will be a small period of calm. The graph dips slightly as you come to the denouement, which is simply the period of explanation before the satisfying finale to all that has gone before.

The climax of a novel is not always the actual end of it. A climax suggests excitement, the highest peak of attainment, the kind of adrenalin rush that would leave readers high and dry if there was nothing to follow. This works particularly well in twist-ending short stories, where the clever and sudden punchline ending is the aim of the story.

But in a novel the true climax usually comes just before the end, leaving readers time to catch their collective breath before everything is tied up as neatly as the particular novel demands.

Think of the crime novel where the detectives are

explaining their brilliant methods of deduction. This is not the climax. The climax has already happened, when the villain was caught and the detectives emerge triumphant. The explanations don't detract one iota from the enjoyment of the book, or give a sense of let-down. Instead, they enhance it.

Or the romance, where the lovers declare their feelings after the tortuous doubts and misunderstandings and anti-climaxes you have put them through. Romance readers need to enjoy their mutual happy ending, and savour it, but the climax to the book happened when the stars were finally in the lovers' eyes. It is what romance editors call the *raison d' être* of the genre book.

Or the science fiction novel, where your heroes have come down to earth after traumatic and hazardous journeys into outer space, encountering aliens and space storms of gigantic proportions, and conquering them all in a terrific climax. They are then greeted by a welcoming committee amid huge national pride and acclaim. Readers need this touch of calm after the storm, and so do the characters in order to reap all their just rewards.

Get to know where you want your book's climax to occur. And leave time and space at the end of it to convey to the reader that sense of just having finished reading a well-rounded book. There is nothing more annoying than the feeling of 'the cavalry coming over the hill' when you reach the last page, when you find that the author wraps everything up in a few neat sentences. Leave that to the twist-ending short story, and give novel readers their money's-worth.

Time span

All novels have a time span to them. That much is

obvious. And considering your time span when you first think about developing your plot can be one of the easiest ways for the beginner to start. Once you do this, you have parameters to work within. Your characters must achieve their goals and aspirations within certain time-limits. And you can plan and pace your plot accordingly.

Maybe in your planned story danger looms if the characters do not meet their deadline; or an important power struggle will come to nothing unless it is accomplished within a certain time. Many a historical novel has been created on the premise of an inheritance becoming due on a particular date and the characters having to fulfil some quest by the due date or lose the lot.

Marriage of convenience plots are a natural theme here. Claiming an inheritance on a certain date could also be a strong incentive to murder. Use your imagination to see how the use of the time span can aid your plot.

I have written some of my historical novels with a one-year time span, bringing the novel full circle by means of the changing seasons. I have also written several teenage novels with a 48-hour time span in confined atmospheres, which stretched my imagination and ingenuity.

You might want to work on a much larger canvas, time-wise. There are many other things to think about if this is the case. My long saga *All in the April Morning* took my characters from the San Francisco earthquake of 1906 to the end of the Second World War. This was not done by chance. In terms of time I knew how far I wanted to take them from the outset, and I paced the action accordingly.

Covering a longer length of time involves a lot of research, as I also had to take into account the changing decades, national and international events, fashion, transport, communications, and so on. Research will be dealt with in more detail in the next chapter.

Dramatic as that earthquake was, if I had written three-quarters of *All in the April Morning* detailing it, then rushed the characters through the Second World War, the book wouldn't have worked at all. In fact, the earthquake, although a devastating event, took up a very small proportion of the beginning. Its purpose was to act as the catalyst for the remainder of the book and, in particular, the effect it had on the central character. The plot had to balance.

Another of my sagas, *Scarlet Rebel,* dealt with fictional characters involved in the Jacobite Rebellion, and the parameters of Bonnie Prince Charlie's fourteen months in Scotland gave me a very useful time span for my novel. Use every trick available to you, providing it makes good sense.

Summary

- Don't give everything away at once in your plot.
- Balance and pace the action.
- Think of your plot as a jigsaw. Make the pieces fit.
- Check the acceptable length of your type of novel.
- Use time span to your plotting advantage.

6

THE CHAIN REACTION

Before you break rules, you had better learn them
Noel Coward

Writing a successful novel where everything reads so smoothly that it seems as if the author had an effortless task is no accident. You might as well get used to the fact that most non-writers believe that you sit in front of the screen all day long, and the words just flow out, ready-formed and in perfect shape and order. You wish!

Occasionally – *very* occasionally, they do. But far more often, it's a long hard slog to achieve that effect. Sentences need to be changed around, repetitive words and phrases removed, paragraphs tightened, and so on. And throughout all this process is the hope that you are going to produce a saleable novel at the end of it. It takes work.

The novel that has the most chance of success has a plot that has a chain reaction effect. Nothing in it is out of context. Everything leads on from what has gone before, even in the most complex plot – and no matter how many twists and turns there are. Extraneous characters who are incidental to the plot and do not belong there are cut out. Waffling asides and author-intrusion while you air one of your particular little hobby-horses are *definitely* out. Novels are about the characters the author creates, not about the author.

Chapters and scenes

While there are few rules that can't be broken by a sparkling and innovative writer, I do believe that if you truly want to see your book in print, then some of the basics are vital. The use of chapters and scenes may be obvious, but occasionally writers have tried to change the recognised format, with varying reactions from readers.

Separating your book into chapters is pleasing to the eye as well as giving you and the reader time to pause for breath. Chapters are also essential for:

- Separating locations.
- The progression of time, weather or seasons.
- Changing viewpoints where applicable.

There was a brief fashion for writing novels without any chapter divisions, or by making them so short that they were no more than one page long in some instances.

Both of these methods are gimmicky. I don't believe that many readers really appreciated them, and I certainly don't think they are attractive to write. A novel with one long endless amount of prose from page 1 to page 300, or whatever, gives the impression of a flat, one-dimensional story. It's like being involved in a one-sided 'conversation', where the other person never gives you a chance to have your say. And don't we all know about *them*!

Alternatively, the habitual one-page-chapter book, which could presumably run to hundreds of mini-chapters (Does the author dare to number them? Some do) can only result in bitty, characterless writing. This is my opinion, and there are doubtless people who will disagree with me. So, if this is the way you want to write your book, the best of luck with it.

Most writers will stick to the tried and trusted methods, but that is not to say that every chapter in the novel has to be the same length. Of course not. It all depends on how the book is progressing and how dramatic each chapter is intended to be, but also on the type of book you are writing.

A short genre romance novel will usually require, say, ten or twelve chapters of fairly consistent length, and a publisher of the genre won't look kindly on the occasional chapter that is merely two pages long. Other books, less rigid in their requirements, will sometimes take such a chapter in the middle of more regularly constructed ones, especially if it is of some catalystic impact, or significant character involvement. A stark contrast to longer chapters can be useful for shock value, providing it is appropriate to the plot.

Chapters are not the same as scenes, although a chapter may consist of an entire scene; that is, the same set of characters are engaged in some kind of dialogue and action that takes up the entire twenty pages or whatever.

Or a chapter may contain several scenes, which break up the chapter into smaller chunks, but are always relevant to that chapter's progress. Scene changes are always indicated by an extra line space in the text, and if you are uncertain about this method, study any published novel.

Try to always think in scenes when writing the novel, whether the scene comprises a whole chapter, or is a shorter piece within that chapter. Scenes are complete in themselves, as when two characters are having a blistering row – and this may be lengthy or consist of less than half a page. Although if it was a *really* blistering row, I would expect it to go on for longer – and so would readers. I wouldn't advise too many tiny scenes within a chapter anyway, or you are back to bittiness again.

But while scenes are complete in themselves, and could be considered as mini-chapters, they are also part of the whole. The most effective scenes are those that have grown out of the ones that come before it.

This linking effect is vital in any good plot. A chapter too is always linked in some way to the one that has gone before, and the one that comes after it. If it does not, then you might as well be writing a dozen short stories, instead of writing something that is a cohesive whole ...

Holding up the action by design

... Unless, of course, you are holding up the action deliberately. This is a well-known technique which keeps readers in suspense, and encourages them to read on. It is the technique successfully employed in television soap operas, when the story-lines involve a large cast of characters, and several small stories are interwoven. This is the key word. The stories are *interwoven*.

An example: my novel *Wives, Friends and Lovers* told the story of three girls and their interwoven lives. Chapters were written from various angles, sometimes Laura's, sometimes Gemma's, sometimes Penny's. The three were closely involved with one another, so there was always a chapter in which at least two of them were linked.

But the changing viewpoint when dealing more with Gemma than Laura, for instance, pulled the reader up sharply and threw a curve into the plot. Occasionally, the scenes within the chapters also switched viewpoints, and there is also a technique to follow here to keep the action smooth. Again, study the novels where such changing viewpoints within chapters is employed. It is not for the faint-hearted.

So, a word of warning. When you write scenes within chapters, avoid too many viewpoint changes to avoid bittiness. If your scene is shown through a new character's viewpoint, indicate it quickly, so that readers aren't confused by thinking the same character is controlling the action.

This also applies to the beginning of a chapter. Always make sure your reader knows who is taking charge of the action by bringing in the character's name as quickly as possible. In a novel where the central viewpoint character is always the same one, then this advice does not apply.

- Plot your individual chapters and scenes with as much attention to detail and variety as the whole novel.
- Throwing curves to what the reader is expecting can also refresh and sustain reader interest.

Cliffhangers

Every chapter worth its salt ends on a cliffhanger. A reckless statement, perhaps. But the reason for including them at all is not only to give continuity to the plot, but also to induce readers to read on and *see what happens next*. It keeps them in suspense. It is the hook to catch your fish.

In a novel where several viewpoints are used, and where a new chapter may begin with a different viewpoint character taking control, this holds up the suspense still more, and enhances this need for readers to read on. It is the stuff of family sagas where many diverse family members may be involved in the plot. But there are cliffhangers and cliffhangers ...

The most dramatic kind live up to their job description, and literally leave the characters hanging over the edge of the proverbial cliff; or with the villain's hands choking the life out of the victim; or seeing the alien space-ship racing towards the lunar module with no chance of diverting it; or the female character finding the rapist waiting for her in a darkened alley; or the business executive realising that his fraudulent conversion of funds into a Swiss bank account has been discovered.

All of these scenarios would provide good, meaty cliffhangers. Yet there is a less dramatic but nonetheless effective kind of cliffhanger, depending on the kind of novel you are writing. Consider the following cliffhangers:

- The poignant moment when a woman returns from her lover's funeral to find a post-dated letter from him.
- The sick panic of pot-holers when they finally know there is no way out and the underground water level is rising.
- The romantic heroine's realisation that she loves the hero after all, and it may be too late ...
- The family saga where estranged family members are reunited in an uneasy atmosphere for whatever occasion the story demands.
- The society wedding where someone speaks up and denounces the bridegroom as a bigamist.
- The car plunging over the cliff ... surely the *ultimate* cliffhanger!

Apart from the last, most of those are more emotional

than action-filled cliffhangers, although the way each scene is written could give whatever interpretation that you wished, and all of them can have dramatic potential.

The point of all of them is that readers will be left with a huge question-mark in their minds, thus compelling them to read on to the next chapter ... and the next.

And the vital question is: *What is going to happen next, and what are the characters going to do about it*? If you refer to each of the examples I have given, you will see that each one puts an almost desperate need in readers' minds to follow it through. In each case, we *care* what is happening to the character concerned, which is why we want to know how he or she is going to react to the situation. This is the power of the cliffhanger in any novel. Don't neglect its importance when working on your plot. And it all forms part of the chain reaction of linking scenes and chapters.

Fitting it all together

Let's catch our breath for a minute. At this point, I want to repeat that my 'numbers method' – of suggesting 20 chapters for your book – was not meant to imply that you should have 20 chapters at all, or that this is the desired number for any book. Far from it. It was merely an example.

You can have any number of chapters that you like, with certain reservations that I have already mentioned, for example, in Harlequin Mills & Boon contemporary novels. Writing is a personal, creative occupation, aside from the dictates of publishers – which also applies to the cost of paper and printing and other things that don't directly concern you but have to be taken into consideration. But what is comfortable for you is always going to be your best method of working and planning, the one that will produce the best results.

But don't ever lose sight of the one over-riding aspect of what will make your book publishable. Nothing will guarantee that more than good writing, and I will put my neck on the line and say that you could read How To books until eternity and never achieve publication. You could attend every conference and workshop there is, and listen avidly to every published author and tutor, and make endless notes and fill those notebooks with their sound advice. You could probably write your own How To book by now by using all the masses of notes you've accumulated, and still never get published.

And why not? It could be because you haven't assimilated the one vital thing that makes a novel a page-turner. You haven't become a story-teller. It's not enough to know the individual parts that go into the making of a novel if you can't fit it all together into something that others find interesting, and are willing to pay money for.

So. Let's start putting the separate components into some kind of order, and then think about fitting it all together. Let's go back to the beginning. Let's have a story to tell.

Fact and fiction in partnership

Where do you begin? Character or plot – or both? Remember that however brilliantly you have devised your plot, you need strong and memorable characters to carry that plot through. One is dependent on the other. One is part of the other. One enhances, develops and resolves the other. In a novel, one without the other doesn't even exist.

Fact and fiction are interwoven in all plots. Even if the facts are little more than the streets of your home town that you know well and can describe without moving away from your word processor, and the characters are brilliant figments of your imagination, you have involved fact and fiction.

We are not concerned here with biographies or non-fiction books. Novels are fiction, involving fictional characters and fictional events, unless they are set against a national or specific historical background. But without checking those facts to prove their worth and to back up your fictional story, mistakes can still reduce your novel to nonsense and take away the writer's credibility.

You don't believe it? I once read a novel by a reputable author who described the long sandy beach at Sorrento. Anyone who has ever been there, or who had the gumption to read a travel brochure as the simplest way to check on it, knows that there is no long sandy beach at Sorrento. There will be many readers who don't know this – and you may think that the editor should have known it, or had it checked – but it was firstly the writer's responsibility to get it right.

I strongly believe that checking facts is an unavoidable part of the plotting process of your novel. It can *help* in the process, as well as hinder it. The small discrepancy above may not have affected the general romance tone of that particular novel, but it would have affected knowledgeable readers' enjoyment of it, causing them to pause instantly, and to mentally register that *that isn't right*.

That's how I felt when I read that book, and you don't want that to happen when someone is reading one of yours. I speak from experience, because I've made mistakes myself, and it's maddening to have it pointed out at a later date. It's maddening for your own integrity, and because you know you should have known better.

And the most maddening thing of all is that a reader who points out the tiniest mistake will often forget to mention how much she enjoyed the other marvellous, 54,999 correct words in the novel. Such is human nature ... and the banana-skin syndrome. You slipped; she didn't.

Making sure that your characters live and breathe in the right era and setting for your novel is one of the obvious ways of getting it right for the reader's enjoyment. No eighteenth century heroine, for instance, would pick up the telephone to speak to her beloved, because it hadn't been invented. This is an extreme and obvious example, but it's perilously easy to get things wrong, and thus lose authenticity in your novel. This is where research comes in.

Essential research

Research is a word that unnerves many beginner writers. After all, it screams of Bloody Hard Work, spending hours in some dusty old museum or poring over endless archives in obscure libraries, and having to travel far and wide to find out some small fact that may not appear more than once in your novel.

Some writers will tell you airily that they never research at all, or that if they do, it is only minimal research. Oh yes? So when you're remembering how you lived it up in the 60s, and are writing about pop festivals and flower power and the like – aren't the memories you're drawing on as much a part of research as studying historical tomes?

I don't think any novelist writes a book without doing some kind of research, however slight. How much time you devote to it is another thing, because it can be time-consuming, frustrating, fascinating and addictive.

Whenever I give a talk on research, it sometimes surprises people to hear me say how research can work for you, giving you twists and turns

for your plot that weren't evident at first. This is what I call 'accidental research' as opposed to intentional research, which is the kind that you do when you know exactly what you want to look up.

This might simply be historical dates and details of dress codes, or chronological data regarding battles and so on. It might be checking on the pecking order in the police force hierarchy, which can be as easily done as checking through the cast lists in certain programmes in the *Radio Times*.

My criterion is always to do your research in as easy a way as you can. Which is why I don't believe you *necessarily* need to travel to darkest Borneo to know what it would be like to live there, although I would probably do so if I could. But there are ways and means of finding out such information.

Ask someone who knows whenever you can. Ask someone who once lived in darkest Borneo ... ask people to describe their job to you, whether you want your character to be a deep sea diver, or a district nurse, or whatever. Write to commercial firms for information on industries, stating your reason, and you will almost always be sent masses of background material.

And among all this intentional research there will inevitably be some snippet of information that you just know will enhance or enliven a scene or chapter in your book, or even turn your whole thinking around, because it will make such a spectacular difference to its outcome. In other words, it will help to develop and strengthen your plot.

It has happened to me many times ... in writing *The*

Bannister Girls my hero was in the Royal Flying Corps and in France during the First World War. Finding out as much as I could about the RFC, I discovered that while George V was in France on an inspection tour, a horse reared up in front of him, startling him and the young airmen on parade.

I made sure my RFC hero was there to see it. It was not at all unlikely that he would witness the event, since I could have my hero posted anywhere I chose. And such postings would often be in secret locations for security reasons.

This was a case of fact and fiction intertwined in one small incident that added to the believability of my novel, and only came about because I found it accidentally.

Always be flexible when you find a research point that can be *logically* incorporated in your plot. But never twist history to suit it. Be sure the facts are right, and in a case such as I've described be sure that your characters could be in the right place at the right time.

Similarly, don't describe a real person in a way that documented works record otherwise. Don't change their colouring, height, weight or personality to suit your plot.

Be sure you know when things were first invented, or came into common use. This is all too easy to get wrong, and it's useful to consult a book on the subject, such as *The Shell Book of Firsts*.

I will repeat that my advice is to do as much research as is reasonable for your plot outline, and then get on with writing your book, or you will spend all your time researching and not writing. If that's what you want to do, of course, then who am I to suggest otherwise?

But as long as you are prepared to revise and edit your work –which you must be – then you can always fill in the gaps, providing the missing pieces do not hinge on some vital part of the plot. I simply think it is wasted time to ponder for days or weeks over some small point that can easily be filled in at a later stage.

And if you never thought that an entire plot can be created out of a single basic fact (large oaks from little acorns, etc.), then maybe you should be writing non-fiction. Harsh words? I don't think so. I also know that non-fiction writers will tell me the same thing works for them. Find the spark of an idea, and from then on, it's up to you.

But the key to writing good *fiction* in which you are involving factual information, is to choose an important or significant event –*one that has legs*, to use the weirdest term I know – and then fictionalise it with your own strong characters.

Creating any fictional historical plot that is based on dramatic fact, for instance, will produce something far more readable than one that has been disparagingly called a 'fancy-dress historical'. The simple reason is that you have all those true events at your disposal against which to place your characters ... you have the parameters against which to time span your plot, whether it's the six days of the National Strike or the four years of the First World War ... you have real people whose entry into your plot, whether in a small or large extent, will add colour and richness and authenticity to your novel ... and yes, I actually *love* research, which undoubtedly helps ...

A final comment on the subject is attributed to the wife of Arthur Hailey, about the research for his novel *The Final Diagnosis*: 'He watched open heart surgery, listened to radiologists, pathologists, anaesthetists, talked with nurses, interns, hospital directors.'

Now that's dedication for you, and is the mark of the true professional at work, intent on getting things right. You might also care to know that Hailey's novel *Hotel* is required reading for trainee hotel managers in the USA. So I guess he researched that pretty well too.

If you want to know more about the subject of how to go about it, and where to find a host of research sources from the simple to the obscure, try my *How to Research Your Novel*.

Summary

- Novels are about characters, not you.
- Scenes and chapters should be linked.
- Throw your readers a curve now and then.
- Cliffhangers lure the reader on.
- Don't twist recorded data to suit your plot.
- Get it right!

N.B.   The Internet is also a major source of research, but it's wise to cross-check any facts.

7

BREAKING DOWN THE EPIC PLAN

Writing novels is a way of living alternative lives
Melvyn Bragg

Every novel has a shape to it, which has come about because of the way it has been plotted and graphed, and then written to the best of the author's ability. This shape and planning will not be instantly obvious to the reader who picks it up in a bookshop or library and decides it might be worth reading.

But will it? Only you and your editor know that at this stage. You will have put your heart and soul into it. The editor will have put her faith in it. The publisher will have put money into it. We all want some feedback. We all want to have our passion in this book proved so that the editor will be phoning daily to ask about your next book, and the publisher will be falling over himself to keep you on his list, and agreeing to up your next advance to astronomic proportions because of the huge sales on this first book. Well, all writers are dreamers, aren't they?

So let's get real. Let's get down to the nitty-gritty of what that book needs to make it not only a saleable proposition, but a book that's going to get your foot in the publishing door and launch you on to a career that is just as exciting as you ever thought it could be.

And that's not an idle dream. It happens. The mystique and sense of glamour that comes from the thought of actually *getting into print* is in all our hearts when we first get that burning desire to write, and I don't believe anyone who tells me differently. And when it actually happens ...

Whether you're a dreaded mid-list author with no more than modest but steady sales, or an acclaimed best-selling author of Jackie Collins or Bernard Cornwell status – or a strong library author, as I have rather peculiarly been described – the excitement that comes from seeing your book in print is immense. It never goes away, either, no matter how many books you have published. But, as in all things, you have to take that first step that opens the door.

Your new Best Friend

The first person to see your novel, or any part of it, (leaving aside family, friends and writing circle critics) is going to be an editor. So let's consider the editor. Oh boy, do you need to consider the editor!

This editor, your new Best Friend, who almost certainly doesn't know you – although you will have found out her name and addressed her accordingly, won't you? – will have certain expectations from you. She needs to know that you are going to plunge straight into the theme of the book, so that she is going to be immediately drawn into the world you are creating.

She needs to know that you are going to start, or have started, this book on a high point, maybe a scene of action or an interchange of dialogue between the main characters. She needs to be assured that when a reader picks up this book out of the mass of paperbacks on every bookshop's shelves, this one will intrigue her from page one.

And why should you bother yourself with all this, when you're on some higher plane writing the Great

British Novel? Because she won't buy it if you don't, kiddo.

So when you are devising your plot outline, think about this editor, your new Best Friend, who is waiting avidly, or boredly, for the next batch of unsolicited manuscripts to land on her desk on a wet Monday morning after a rave-up weekend that has left her with an almighty hangover and a commuting journey into her office of nightmare proportions.

(Okay, they're not all like that, but this is fiction, and she's my imaginary editor ... play along, can't you?)

So to continue ...

And here are you: some unknown, faceless author she's never heard of, presenting her with a manuscript of an epic novel that may or may not be rubbish, but which, to her credit, she feels committed to take a look at, just in case. As I said, she's my imaginary editor ... but you never know, this one just might be the next *War and Peace*, and since editors can dream too, this is what she will hope to find in the package you have sent her, together with return postage in case the unthinkable happens, and it is rejected.

There will be a short covering letter, stating the theme of the novel with the approximate number of words, appropriate to the publishing house's requirements; a nicely presented synopsis, condensing the plot in a sharply written, sequential way, and *telling her the ending*.

There will be the first three chapters of the book, not random ones chosen because you rather like the action in Chapter 10, and you know in your heart that Chapters 2 and 3 are a bit dull, ho hum ... or there will be the entire novel if you prefer to send the lot on spec. Some writers do, and there's nothing wrong in doing so if you are happier with that approach. It can certainly throw you into a panic if an editor phones to say that she likes your first three chapters and synopsis and wants to see the entire book ... and you haven't written any more of it yet!

Just remember that whatever you send her, this is your sales package, your intro to a world where success or failure can hinge on a great many external things, including what's saleable at the moment, what's currently in fashion, sending your work to the correct publishing house and, most of all, your plot and your writing style. Many a new writer has been depressed and dejected to get a novel sent back after working on it for many months, but the most important words that an editor, your new Best Friend, can put in her letter to you is *that she would like to see more of your work.*

I know far too many writers who have ignored those vital words, and think that it's just a softener. Almost always, it's not. Editors simply don't have the time for that kind of response, and nor do they invite unlikely authors to try again unless they can see there is some potential in them.

Remember the vast amount of competition you're up against in submitting anything these days, when everyone in the world believes in the old adage that they have a book in them. They probably do, and in most cases it's far better to let it stay exactly where it is.

So if you get this kind of encouragement from an editor, however small it seems at the time, for goodness' sake act on it, and try again. Here endeth the lesson.

Sharp beginnings

Start your plotting on a high point. Make it an important incident that is going to take your readers immediately into your imaginary world, and introduce your main character(s) as quickly as possible. It's been said before, and I'm saying it again, that I sometimes think of it as comparing two paintings that are almost identical.

One painting is of the most beautiful scenery imaginable, and the second one has a figure or group of figures superimposed on that background. Only the most insensitive person would see which painting has the most life about it and which one would intrigue the viewer to wonder about those people and why they are there.

It's the same in a novel. Get your characters *doing* something as quickly as possible. If they are moving on somewhere, get them moving at the beginning of the plot. Don't spend pages letting them think about it. This merely shows indecision on their part. Main characters need some backbone – or what qualifications makes them main characters anyway?

If they have some problem to solve (and again, if not, what are they doing in your book at all?), let the readers in on it. If it is a more static scene let your characters be observing it, or part of it, or having something to say about it. *Get them in the picture.*

Check out this publishing hype on an ad for *Moon Island*, a novel by Rosie Thomas – 'Rosie Thomas's moving [new] novel will draw you into it and will not let you go.' That's the type of reaction to aim for, and it all came about from the way the book began. 'Drawing the readers in ...'

A novel is a three-way thing. Forget the editor and publisher for the moment, because we all know they have their part to play, and once a novel is accepted for publication, many other people will have their fingers in your pie. The particular three-way thing I'm referring to now is between you and your book before it even gets beyond the plotting stage.

- The importance of the characters can't be emphasised enough. But there are two others involved in this affair.
- There is you, the author who created them, and who is guiding them through the plot.
- There is the reader, who has the same kind of expectations as the editor, and has every faith in your plot.

So what are you giving this reader, who wants to believe totally in the lies you are telling her ...?

I've said a dirty word now. Lies. But if we're completely honest (!) about it, fiction is all lies, isn't it? Lies or invention or fantasy, or that peculiar suspension of disbelief. Call it what you will. And call it entertainment too. And therapy. And escapism. And having got all that out of the way, and not caring a jot which word you prefer to use, back to the basics.

Start with a good sharp beginning. Plunge into your story so that the reader is in no doubt what it is going to be about. Give your chapters cliffhanger endings, which you may prefer to call hooks. Whatever you call them, intrigue readers enough so that they feel compelled to read on. Get started. Above all, be passionately interested in the story you're going to tell. If you're not completely involved in it, and in the lives of these imaginary people you've created, why the hell should anybody else be?

If you want your readers to believe in what you're telling them, firstly believe in it yourself.

And then, after that wonderful beginning, maybe when you've outlined the plan for those first few chapters or even got farther into the book, almost everyone comes to a point when they think: where do I go from here?

Transitions and sagging middles

In the last chapter, the scenes and chapters of your novel were discussed, including cliffhangers and hooks to link each one of these to the next. You may think that these transitions should always be smooth, seemingly effortless on the part of the author – despite the amount of planning that has gone into producing just that effect – and taking the reader along to the next part of their journey through the plot.

This is not always so. Sometimes the transition from scene to scene – and from chapter to chapter – can be startling, reviving readers' interest if it should be in danger of flagging (surely not ...)

A plot transition is no more than a shifting of emphasis from one angle to another, from one character's viewpoint to another, or from a change in time or location or mood. But, as in all things, variety makes for interest, and the plot that meanders along on the same old winding road without any humps or bumps in its path can be pretty boring. Using transitions that vary the mood and the pace of the novel can enliven a story-line considerably, and when you are plotting the route of your novel, you should keep these possibilities in mind.

It's horrible to get to a point in your novel when you can't think where to go next. You have reached the sagging middle of your plot, and all seems dull and pointless. You're quite sure this novel is never going to be finished, that you will finally abandon it and that it will end up in the drawer with all the other unfinished manuscripts. You are not alone. But hold on. Because the most important word in your vocabulary now is **Choice.**

Think about your plot so far. You will have created a set of characters, a solid background, you know where the story will begin and where it will end. But oh, that sagging middle section is where you actually have to keep the interest going, to stop the editor reaching for the padded, self-addressed envelope that you sent her ...

To offset the risk of that happening, and before that book is abandoned before it even gets to the editor's desk, let's go back and dissect the elements more thoroughly. And all of the following thoughts will not only pep up that sagging middle, but will help towards ...

Thickening the plot

The characters

You have created them and profiled them, and you know them well. But do you know everything about them? Is there something in their make-up that you have not yet exploited? Can you add something to their profile that you hadn't thought of in the beginning, that will enrich them? If they are too saintly, maybe a few extra flaws would be in order; too dastardly, maybe there is yet a saving grace waiting to pop up.

Being all black or all white, temperamentally speaking, makes the characters as boring as if they are all an indeterminate grey. We all have secrets, however small, however slight. Let them have secrets too – and regarding fictional characters, remember that the secrets could be major, and well out of sight, until ...

Think where they might go in the plot, and how they might react if something totally unforeseen happened to them, which isn't character-promoted but outside their province. An earthquake, a storm, a win on the lottery, a financial disaster in the family, a tragic accident, a burglary, a mugging, a fatal illness, an offer they can't refuse.

What that offer is, would be up to you and your plot. A love affair, perhaps? The chance to work abroad for a year? A change of identity for whatever reason?

The possibilities for propping up sagging middles are endless, if you use your imagination and ensure that any one of the above does not happen as the result of chance, but as a logical progression to the plot.

A solid background

You will already have determined this before you began working on your plot. Make sure you have explored all the possibilities that this background offers you in terms of plot movement. If it is a quiet country setting, maybe the setting for a murder or two ... have you chosen a real place, or a fictional one, which is by far the safer?

If you have created your own country setting, have you drawn a map of the place, so that you know exactly how far each building is from the next, and how long it would take your villain to do his work? Any copper and forensic expert worth their salt would take these things into account, so it's up to you to do your homework in the first place. Credibility is the name of the game.

And as an aside ... years ago I wrote a regular series of short stories for a magazine under the name of Dr Grant. These were warm, character-driven stories, and Dr Grant was merely the fictional storyteller in a small town. But – and here is the point – I was provided with a mass of information from the publisher about this fictional town, streets and buildings etc., so that everything fitted from week to week.

Nothing was left to chance, and this small town really

lived in the imagination, and I know from the letters I received via the magazine that readers believed that it really did exist. That's what I mean by knowing your background and believing in it.

Such attention to detail can be applied to whatever kind of fiction you are writing, and whatever plot you devise. Maeve Binchy says that when she begins a book she draws a map of the imaginary village or town, and details in it the important buildings, shops, bars, cafes, and so on. It all helps to recreate the scene of the story so that readers can see what she is seeing in her imagination.

Where your story begins

Once you have actually begun to write your book and are into your first chapter, you may wonder how you are going to make a 100,000-page book out of a few pages of plot outline. This is where the danger of unnecessary expansion to 'set the scene' is most evident. Take a long look at your first few pages and then compare it with your plot outline.

It's quite common to begin at the wrong point, to take a little time 'getting into the story' before you get to the real beginning, the part where the characters assume life and tell the reader what their story is all about. Be ruthless in that long hard look at the beginning and see if you have waffled too much, and if the story really starts a couple of pages on. If the answer is yes, then be just as ruthless about discarding those first few paragraphs or pages if need be.

This is where referring to your plot outline is invaluable, because when you first devised it, you knew exactly where you wanted your story to begin and where you wanted it to end. Keeping that reference in mind, check the beginning and ending again.

Where your story ends

I always think of a novel as a journey, where you are taking the characters along a pre-planned route until they reach their satisfactory ending, the one that will please you and the characters and the readers. That threesome again ...

Check the ending in your plot outline. Is it logical? If it is so unlikely that it makes the rest of the book seem ludicrous, no editor will consider it. You have probably seen as many publishers' hypes about new novels as I have, saying that the ending will shock and amaze you. This is not only a ploy to make readers buy the book, it is a compliment to the authors' ingenuity in producing such an ending.

But is the ending to your book still logical? In other words, no matter how incredible, fantastic, unexpected, and all those other words that mean virtually the same thing in this context, if it is not logical to the nature of the characters themselves, then it will not work.

Plots can and should be full of unexpected twists and turns, so that readers are always kept wondering what is going to happen next, but the ending should always provide them with that sense of having read a damn good book.

Compare your beginning with your ending. Your characters should have developed through their strengths and weaknesses and whatever encounters they meet before their journey through the pages is brought to a satisfactory conclusion. Not every book ends with a triumphant and rip-roaring scene of action, but the ending of it should be right for its genre, its sense of time and place, and most of all, for the characters involved in it.

Twists and turns

Assuming that you are taking a second or third look at where you can liven up your plot, especially with regard to that sagging middle, consider the twists and turns carefully.

Being logical doesn't rule out the fact that something unexpected can crop up. Suggestions:

- The uninvited dinner guest.
- The illegitimate child appearing on the doorstep.
- The letter from a distant relative claiming the inheritance you thought was safely yours.
- The phone call with a disguised voice that you recognise with a feeling of dread.
- The stolen credit card bill.
- The shock of seeing a past lover or spouse whom you believed was dead ...

All of those things might happen in a novel and would provide plenty of changes of direction in your plot. But would they be acceptable to readers? They certainly would – *if your characterisation was such that these events were perfectly possible in their lives.*

Basing your twists and turns on how you have profiled your characters will add new dimensions to your plot. It will help to make those characters as real and as vulnerable as we all are when faced with something unexpected. And huge successes and triumphs can be as nerve-racking as any other kind of shock, although clearly with different outcomes.

The clues to such twists and turns must already be there, and the clues will often come through the characters themselves. If you have shown, briefly, that your mild-mannered man is prone to violent rages that he normally keeps well contained within himself, would it not be logical then for this violence to erupt into murder? And would not your normally mild-mannered man help the police with their enquiries as best he could, until his Achilles heel was eventually discovered by astute police detection and clever questioning to trap him? – thus keeping the punters reading to see when he will give the game away and get his come-uppance.

Twists and turns in the plot shouldn't depend on coincidence. We all know they happen in real life but, oddly enough, they never seem to work in fiction. Nobody has ever given a satisfactory explanation for this, but every writing tutor I have ever listened to has said the same thing. It's a pity really, because coincidence used to be rife in the classics, when we were not so sophisticated as we are now, and coincidences were completely accepted by readers.

I suspect that some clever academic decided that authors weren't doing a proper job if they relied on coincidence to solve all their characters' problems. I don't disagree with that, but could your romantic heroine *never* decide on the spur of the moment to go to London for the day, and accidentally bump into an old flame? Of course she could. It's the stuff of *Brief Encounter* after all, and who can forget the coincidental meeting of Celia Johnson and Trevor Howard in a railway station buffet ... aahhhh ...

If I was using that kind of scenario or so-called accidental meeting in a plot of my own, I would have indicated the heroine's compulsive, unpredictable nature, and ensured that the old flame had a special reason for being where he was on that particular day. In other words, the clues would be there ... so perhaps the clever academic had something after all, in making us *think* before we put it all down to coincidence, so that it didn't seem like coincidence at all.

Summary

- Believe in your characters and plot.
- Don't let your novel sag in the middle.
- Provide twists and turns that are logical.
- Don't rely on coincidence.

8

SUSTAINING THE PACE

The secret of getting ahead is getting started
Mark Twain

The use of pace (as opposed to pacing out the action) in any novel is a sure way of involving readers in the plot. We've all heard the phrase 'a fast-paced novel' and occasionally 'a plot that leaves the reader breathless'. Both of these publishing blurbs are meant to persuade you not to stop reading the book until you get to the end, and that the author has written a terrific page-turner.

This is great – especially if that author is you. But is it? And even if your style of writing doesn't allow for this galloping rush through the pages, remember that pace is an adaptable word than can be interpreted on various levels.

Make sure that the pace you put into your plot is the one that you intend, and the one that the readers will pick up. It can mean fast or slow, heart-stopping – or pedantically plodding. If your idea of pace is that of a snail attempting to climb Mount Everest, forget it.

But I know it isn't. Not if you've read this far, anyway! You know all about the importance of pace by now, and how it is always moving the plot forward through action and dialogue and the interaction of the characters and their problems. The difficult bit is how to sustain that pace.

Even in the lustiest blood-and-thunder novel, the pace can't *always* be at razor-sharp pitch. A kitchen-sink drama can't *always* have the characters wallowing in domestic hiatus, violence and pathos.

Nor can a romantic novel *always* support a love scene every ten or twenty pages. (Oh no, it can't, and it doesn't, so don't believe those genre sneerers who tell you otherwise – they are usually readers who haven't read a romantic novel for years, anyway.)

But since variety means added vitality ... always try to vary the pace in whatever plot you are devising. Think of pace as something selective that you can use to your advantage; sometimes it will be racing ahead, sometimes it will be less aggressive and more thought-provoking.

Action plots will obviously demand more scenes of a vigorous pace; historical plots may warrant more scenes of a slower, more gracious pace. In every case, the pace of the plot will be pushing the novel forward towards its conclusion.

While all plots must contain conflict and tension if they are not to become completely pedestrian, they also need that variation in the use of pace, otherwise the tension would be unbearable. You couldn't walk a tightrope at full stretch for ever, which is what the effect of a plot of unrelenting pacing would be. You would be exhausted long before you reached the safety net.
REMEMBER TO GIVE YOUR CHARACTERS AND YOUR READERS TIME TO DRAW BREATH.

Keeping up the suspense

Suspense in the plot can be sustained still more by holding up the action in the novel. One way in which this can be achieved is if your novel involves the use of multi-viewpoints. These were referred to briefly in earlier chapters and their usefulness needs to be explained in more detail.

You may ask what their *real* purpose is in furthering

the plot, and whether all of them have the same value in the book? I will explain more a little later on ... and by making you wait in this way, I'm deliberately holding up the action.

Putting the suspense into any novel is just another way of including tension and keeping your readers intrigued. One sure thing is that it must be there.

Suspense doesn't have to be of the blood-curdling variety, unless that is the kind of book you are writing. In horror books it may well be necessary and desirable, but in other kinds of fiction it may be no more than an either/or kind of suspense. Examples:

- Will the new receptionist give in to the persuasive office Romeo, or not? And with what consequences?
- Will your serious-minded researcher take the job of a lifetime in deepest Peru or stick with the safety of his pensionable university post?
- Will the all-action Bond hero manage to save the day in the nick of time, or be thwarted at the last moment?

In that last example, since he's the hero, we *know* he'll win through in the end, but it's the how and the wherefore of achieving his task that keeps up the suspense in the plot. It's the doubts that the author puts in readers' minds as to which way the characters will go.

That sometime favourite-of-the-moment plot, involving the serial killer, has all the chilling elements of suspense. Consider the anxieties that readers will have about him:

- Will he be discovered before he kills again?
- Where and when will the next killing happen?
- Is anyone safe?
- Is there a pattern to the killings?

(And why isn't one of us writing that kind of book right now, with all the possibilities it offers?)

And it is a point worth making that in all novel-writing, you need to put your personal distastes and prejudices aside in the interest of what makes a good plot. It's said that everyone puts something of himself into a plot, but there's nothing to say that you can't be the good guy, is there?

More about multi-viewpoints

And so back to multi-viewpoints. You may not have considered using them at all, or known quite how to use them in your own type of fiction. You may be nervous of trying something new, and yet the use of multi-viewpoints may be just what is needed to enrich your plot.

And just to make it absolutely clear, it is something that is done deliberately, and should be pre-planned when you create your plot. You don't simply switch viewpoints whenever you feel like it, or bring in every character's point of view.

It has to be said that many beginners automatically switch viewpoints haphazardly, without realising that there is a technique to the proper use of viewpoint – which is more simply explained as being the voice of the current narrator.

The result of switching viewpoints willy-nilly is that it all ends up as a gigantic muddle, with the characters becoming so knotted together that readers are left wondering who is talking and who is who. A sure way to stop them reading!

Using multi-viewpoints won't work in every novel that you write, and maybe you won't find them the most effective way to write yours. But they are an option you should be aware of, and the reason I like using them so much is because they give a three- dimensional feel to the novel. You see the events from different angles, and through different eyes.

They are a natural in family sagas, but these are by no means the only novels that can benefit from their use. When you begin creating your plot, my essential advice is to try to determine from the outset how many viewpoints you are going to use in your novel. Too many can get cumbersome.

I have already mentioned my contemporary book *Wives, Friends and Lovers* ... written from three different viewpoints, and how the lives of my three girls were all intertwined. This kind of interaction is what gives variety to the plot, and also a change of pacing, because each of the three girls had different characters and aspirations. I also used the three girls' angle in *The Bannister Girls*.

It could just as easily have been two or four, but there is a limit to the number of multi-viewpoints it is feasible to use, so don't be tempted to use a cast of thousands from which to tell your story. Too many narrators only deflects the importance of the main protagonists.

In each of the above-mentioned books, I *planned* from the beginning that I would explore three diverse personalities. The girls in each plot all had very different routes through the novel, although they were all inevitably linked together. This is what multi-viewpoint is all about.

Also, it had to be clearly defined that all three of them had sufficient importance in the plot, and that two of them were not were not just thrown in as accessories to the central character.

Wives, Friends and Lovers could have been written solely from Laura's viewpoint, but it would not have had the depth of characterisation that three separate viewpoints gave to it.

Each girl could see something in the other two that may not have been evident to themselves. Each, when it became relevant in the plot, became a prop or a hindrance for one or two of the others. And a sounding-board too, which is very useful in giving the reader information. Remember the all-important confidant(e) character.

It's just like life, really, when any group of close friends, family members or colleagues see the good and the bad in each other, and love or hate one another because of it. This is the real value of the multi-viewpoint plot, because it gives richness and depth to what might otherwise be a simple, straightforward storyline.

But you may have noticed that in one of the preceding paragraphs, I only mentioned the name of one of the girls, Laura. This is because, despite the fact that the three friends depended on one another in many ways – and knew so much about each other, Laura was still the central character of the book. She was the one who held the plot together, and it is important that you never lose sight of who you have decided on as your central character. Always know who that character will be, and keep the faith in your own mind.

Sub-plots

If you have never seriously considered using sub-plots in your novel, and are not even sure what they are, then by now you may be thinking that by using multi-viewpoints in a novel you are automatically using sub-plots. And so you are.

Using sub-plots simply means that there are one or more strands of a story weaving in and out of the central one. They do not even necessarily have to involve several characters.

One strongly motivated character may have several strands to his persona. He may be a Mafia king in the exposed, aggressive part of his life, while he may be a caring, different kind of 'godfather' figure to a bunch of orphaned Romanian children.

Such an unlikely facet of his character may be entirely due to the cynical need to offset some of his ill-gotten gains (which you would have plotted in considerably fine detail to make it feasible), but these two differing life-styles, interlinked and maybe inexorably growing closer together with whatever results you planned for this man, would provide you with a sub-plot that would weave in and out of the main one.

Twins separated at birth suggest sub-plotting on a different level, maybe as each one finds (or tries not to find) the other. The reasons, background secrets, lifestyles and eventual outcome of these ideas would make quite a twist told from the two opposing angles. One would almost certainly be the stronger and therefore the natural protagonist and controller of the plot, but the other would be a very threatening (or not) antagonist and provide the sub-plot.

In Jeffrey Archer's *Kane and Abel* the protagonists are not twins but two men born on the same day on opposite sides of the world whose paths are destined to cross in a ruthless power struggle. The stories run side by side, until eventually ... read it and find out for yourselves.

The classics are full of plot and sub-plot. Thomas

Hardy's books invariably involve several rustic men whose stories are all interlinked, lusting after the same innocent country girl. Charles Dickens's books are so densely plotted and full of diverse characters that you can hardly tell where one sub-plot merges into another, and yet you never lose the main thread, nor forget who the story is really about.

- The successful sub-plot weaves a supporting thread throughout the main plot, but never over-shadows it.
- The sub-plot must never be a separate entity, but is always a prop to the main story.
- The central character is always evident.

The variety of pace and character that the sub-plot brings into play furthers the suspense element, which is so vital to reader involvement. It also increases the substance of a plot that may be in danger of being a little thin.

But beware of working out two compatible story-lines about several different sets of characters, in the simple belief that if they run side by side, they will provide you with a substantially long novel. They won't, *unless* each story has some relevance to the other, and promotes it in some way. There must always be that connection.

Pride and Prejudice is a perfect example of the use of sub-plots. Elizabeth Bennet and her sister Jane each have stories of their own, which are family-orientated, and so, eventually, does the silly Lydia during her affair with Wickham. The fact that Wickham has been adversely connected with Darcy only adds more complications and convoluted sub-plots into a complex story of manners and, well, prejudices, which Jane Austen controls beautifully.

If there were no lessons on the craft of writing taught in her day, then a new author can certainly learn a great deal from an instinctive and masterly story-teller.

None of these sub-plots, some of greater importance than others, detract from the impact of the central story-line, which is that of Elizabeth and Darcy's involvement with one another. No one ever forgets that Elizabeth Bennet is the central character in the plot.

Mrs Bennet's comical and eternal quest to find husbands for her daughters brings a slighter but nonetheless important sub-plot into the novel, but all of them enhance and give more weight to the central story-line.

The sub-plot is subsidiary to the main plot, but if you include one at all, then it has to play its part, and is not there as a little aside. Control it, and never let it assume more importance than its role deserves.

My favourite classic author is Thomas Hardy – probably because his novels appeal to my own West Country background – and his *Far from the Madding Crowd* is another prime example of the use of sub-plot.

The central plot clearly concerns Bathsheba Everdene and her future. She is the central character, and the reader is never left in any doubt of this. There are three men in her life (the trilogy crops up again and again in fiction), each of whom has a sub-plot of his own.

- Gabriel Oak who loves her, was once an influential farmer. Having lost his livelihood he is reduced to seeking employment as a shepherd. And guess who has just come up in the world and is looking for such an employee? Bathsheba, of course. Coincidence or what? But so cleverly constructed that it is totally believable.

110

- Then there is the austere, older and richer Mr Boldwood, not really looking for a wife, but intrigued by the mischievous antics of Bathsheba and her maid in sending him a Valentine card.
- Finally there is the randy Sergeant Troy, whose sub-plot with the flighty Fanny Robin might have had nothing to do with the main thread, until he meets the far more desirable Bathsheba, and events take a different turn.
- And just to add more complexity to it all, we learn that Fanny Robin has been a ward of Mr Boldwood and has since disappeared, and she has also been an employee at Bathsheba's newly acquired inheritance.

Sub-plots all, and resulting in a satisfyingly rich plot where everything knits together, despite the sometime doom and gloom of Hardy's writing, with characters that have stood the test of time. May we all be so resourceful.

Planting loose ends

How can you logically introduce a sub-plot that doesn't seem as if you are going off at a tangent from the main plot of the novel? Or throw in a few sentences that don't seem to have any point to them at that moment? Providing you know perfectly well that this *isn't* the case, and that the threads are hanging together, if momentarily separated, then don't be afraid of occasionally doing just that.

Sometimes this shock effect is just what the plot needs, to give the readers a pinch in the arm, so to speak, and get them thinking too. This can occur when the sub-plot involves a change of viewpoint character – remembering that a new chapter and a different angle should always begin by your making it clear who is now in charge of the action.

Involving readers in your story means giving them food for thought, and not dotting every i and crossing every t. And now and then you will deliberately plant loose ends in a chapter, knowing that these loose ends are not going to be picked up until a chapter or so farther on. No problem.

If you are writing with authority and have planned it well, then the readers will have registered the loose end, and when it is picked up and knitted back into the plot, they will accept it.

Example:

David and Karen are on the brink of becoming business partners and are having a furious row, since Karen won't be around for the next week, as she's going to visit her mother, and perhaps they should both think seriously about the wisdom of working together.

(Loose end – how will this be resolved?)

NB: People having rows say things they don't mean, and rarely make long speeches to get their points across.

The next chapter may be dealing with business matters, told mainly from David's viewpoint, and we don't pick up the loose end again until the following chapter.

When we do, Karen is now caring for her mother, who has fallen and broken her leg, which means Karen has to stay with her far longer than expected, and the loose end has been picked up seamlessly.

We are not surprised by it, but there is a new turn of events that is perfectly logical to the plot.

A surprise element may come in here, because

Karen may not be able to contact her partner at this time, or know that the business venture is in danger of falling through without two signatures on the contract.

Maybe she didn't know this at the time, and this could have been left as another loose end.

So what does David do? He might come tearing down to the mother's house, causing conflict between all concerned.

He might decide that business is not all he's interested in, when he sees Karen in a different, more attractive light than that of the tough businesswoman he thought he knew.

The choices would be yours, and this would obviously be a vehicle for a romantic novel, spiced up according to your taste. Loose ends are a vital part of plotting, whatever the category of your novel. The essential thing about them is that they eventually have to be resolved.

Never leave loose ends untied, because dedicated readers will invariably remember them and start wondering what they were doing there. This is a danger when you are plotting detective novels, when there are likely to be a great many loose ends and red herrings to be included and finally resolved. And this alone makes a very good reason for creating a detailed plot before you begin writing the novel.

But loose ends don't *always* have to be planned in advance. You may not even be aware that you are using them ...

Too rigid planning

Maybe after all this you are becoming uneasy about the whole idea of plotting in great detail before you begin to write the novel. The secret is not to be too rigid in your thinking. Always be flexible. Some new idea will almost certainly occur during the actual writing, as and when the characters reveal more of themselves to one another, and also through the events already outlined in your plot. This can happen when you realise you have written something that seems almost out of place and you have no idea why you included it at the time.

Don't let this alarm you. Remember that your plot isn't written in stone. Providing you have a good solid base to begin with, then any small variations or additions to it will almost certainly improve it and give it added depth. If it doesn't, cut it out. It's up to you.

Fiction writers, by their very nature, are imaginative, and the ability to see two sides of every fictional coin is what makes every book different and unique. Keep to the central core of your plot, but don't be afraid to let your imagination provide you with any additional sparks. Leave room for surprises. Think of the simplest romance plot there is:

- boy meets girl
- boy loses girl
- boy gets girl again

This may be the basis of every romantic novel you ever read, but how hideously plodding and mundane it would be if there were no additions, no surprises, no twists and turns, and absolutely no characterisation in those three stark sentences. As it stands, it's bland. It's boring. It hasn't been fully developed. It needs work.

Rejecting the obvious for the unusual

How often have you read a novel and thought how clever that author was – because just when you thought you knew exactly what was going to happen, she managed to surprise you by an unexpected twist? By the final draft of the novel, these things won't have occurred by accident. Even if you have thought your original plot through to your immense satisfaction, there may still be passages where you can give a little surge to the action by questioning your original ideas.

Characters don't always react in the way readers expect them to. For example, your heroine might decide to stay at home instead of going to the cinema. Not much to build on there ...

On the surface this may seem like a pretty feeble twist, if a twist at all, but what if a madman was stalking the block of flats where she lives that night? Does anyone know she had changed her mind? Would someone come looking for her? How would she get out of a tricky and potentially fatal situation? Does she know the stalker?

The obvious may produce a perfectly adequate plot. But the unpredictable can lift it out of the doldrums of adequacy and into the realms of the spectacular.

(I know. Over-writing, but I like it anyway.)

It's a well-known and pretty boring statement that there are only so many basic plots in the world. Maybe. But there must be thousands of variations on them, and it's the way each writer tackles even the best-known plot that gives it the individual touch, and unique voice.

Don't be put off by being told that yours is a Cinderella story that has been done hundreds of times before. It didn't deter Barbara Taylor Bradford (*A Woman of Substance*), or Daphne du Maurier (*Rebecca*), or any of the hundreds of highly successful romantic novelists who conformed to a basic premise, but gave the plot their own magic touch.

And not only that. They took the initial story-line in the Cinderella plot, turned it around, gave it a new twist, a different period in time, a new set of characters. And made each plot individually their own.

This theory of there being only so many plots in the world certainly doesn't stop crime novelists from ensuring that the villain gets his comeuppance, in the time-honoured tradition of the crime genre. *How* they do it is where the skill, ingenuity and imagination comes in. And where allowing the plotting unpredictables – within certain bounds – can pay handsome dividends.

Controlling the plot

But ... however flexible you are in allowing extra elements to enter your original plot, you must still keep tight control of it. Don't let some hitherto unsuspected facet, however exciting, and especially where the characters are concerned, run away with you. They will, given half a chance.

Of course it's thrilling when your characters assume human proportions in your mind – and when you are confident that they are going to do so in your readers' minds. That's what you've been aiming for all this time, and you've done a damn good job when it happens.

And it's very grand, and adds to the mystique of authorship, when you hear writers tell you that the characters take over, and practically write the book themselves ... so that's what you think yours must do for you.

But hold on a minute. While there is a case for saying

the characters will allow you to mentally reject anything they would not say or do, that's fine. And this is due to you – because you have created them so well in your imagination and in your character profiles.

They are still fictional people, and they still exist only in your head. You are still steering them safely through all their raging traumas, and all the horrors you can put them through. They are your creations, part of your book and your plot. *Yours*. Their lives, but your plot.

It's wonderful when the writing is going well, and you are confident that by now you hardly need to look at your plot or synopsis at all. You know exactly where you are going ... and it can be perilously easy to get so carried away by your own writing that these characters, whom you know so well, do the dirty on you, and decide to go their own way.

Far-fetched? Not at all, especially if you are anything of a compulsive writer, and can't wait to get the words out of your head and onto the word processor or whatever. They will lead you into unknown territory if you are not very careful.

Keep control of that plot, and of those characters in particular. Because, yes, they *do* assume lives of their own, and rightly so. If they are to come alive for the readers, they must also come alive for you –and for themselves. They may well want to go down a different track from the one you've outlined for them, and sometimes they're right.

You might take a moment to listen to them – and providing they don't deflect you from your purpose in the overall shape of the plot, you may want to let them have their way – and it may well throw a new dimension into the novel.

But always be aware of your own original plan for your novel. Surprises, twists and turns and new plotting curves are almost all for the good of the plot, but don't let the surprises get out of control. Otherwise you may end up writing a completely different book from the one you intended. And if an editor has already approved the original synopsis, or plot outline, and been so enthusiastic that she has even paid you money up front for it ... need I go on?

Summary

- Sustain the pace in the novel.
- Plots can be enriched through multi-viewpoints.
- Weave in supporting sub-plots.
- Don't leave loose ends untied.
- Leave room for surprises in your plotting.
- Don't let your characters dictate your plot.

9

DISSECTING THE NOVEL

The countless links are strong, that bind us to our clay
Emily Brontë

The above quote, attributed to Emily Brontë, is one that I used in one of the prelim pages of my Rowena Summers novel, *Primmy's Daughter*.

This book is the fifth in a sequence of eight family sagas set in the Cornish china-clay industry, covering nearly a hundred years from the 1850s. The quote seemed appropriate for *Primmy's Daughter*, and was unintentionally relevant to my novel's background. For this book, it also encompasses all that I have said about the links that bind the plot and the characters together.

But in dissecting one of my own novels to show how the plot evolved, I am not going to use *Primmy's Daughter*. Instead, I am using the first book in what has come to be called 'the Clay series': *Killigrew Clay*. It was also the only 'Clay book' I had envisaged at that time.

It was only when it had been published that I saw the rich potential of taking the characters farther on in time. Of course it was possible. Not only that, but now, I believe, inevitable, since those characters already had such a hold on me.

I loved the rich diversity of them all, and the Cornish background was familiar to me. I was writing about a background that I knew – but I soon realised that this was where the general knowledge ended, and the more specific knowledge that would be needed for authenticity in a novel began.

I'm not Cornish, and the extent of my familiarity amounted to the frequency of family holidays over many years. I knew every inch of the Cornish countryside, its insularity, its scented hedgerows, its little coves and inlets and mysterious standing-stones, its history of wrecking and tin-mining, its glorious coastline, that could be so wild and unpredictable, but always magnificent ...

Writing about what I know

I knew all that, but what did I know about china-clay, and why write about that anyway? Commercially, I knew tin-mining had been done to death in fiction, and extremely successfully. The actual name of china-clay didn't have the same ring to it, but there was just as much history about it – and something extra as far as I was concerned.

Anyone who ever went to Cornwall on the 'old roads' knows that almost their first sight of the county before the speedier new roads led you away from it all, were the glinting china-clay spoil heaps. One minute you had no idea of their existence, and then you turned a corner and they loomed up in front of you, stretching into the distance like a ghostly lunar landscape.

For me, this vision alone always set Cornwall apart from anywhere else. Truly a land of magic and mystery, of Merlin and Arthur, and one that went straight to my romantic heart. And the sight of those china-clay sky-tips was the first thing that was imprinted on my mind whenever we visited Cornwall – the moment when we knew we were *there* at last.

As a 'background first' writer, Cornwall was a natural place for me to start. So I would be writing about something I knew. But not well enough. There's a great difference between spending a few weeks as a tourist every year, and utilising that setting for a novel, where everything has to be geographically and aesthetically correct.

And since my idea was for a historical background, set in the heart of china-clay's heyday, it had to be historically correct as well. But by then I knew that my background was definitely going to be in the world of china-clay.

A place called STOP

Now I needed to get these plot thoughts into some kind of order. My theme was nothing fancy or grand. It was simply that of family saga combined with regional industry – which I have used successfully in other novels. For this new book I collated the points I would need, and in no particular order.

They will not all make immediate sense to you – nor did they to me at that point – but they were forming a framework and collection of ideas in my mind, and telling me that there was ample material here for a richly textured plot:

- Background, multi-characters and names.
- Book to begin on a dramatic (and scenic?) point.
- 1850 social conventions to assist the plot.
- Rural occupations, pastimes and superstitions.
- Early conflicts *re* clayworks and family.
- Pointers to further conflict.
- Sub-plots through various family members and subsidiary characters, and through fluctuations of china-clay industry.

- Appeal to the senses *re* Cornish background.
- Use logical situations / clayworkers' strikes, etc. (Check research facts for feasibility).
- Multi-viewpoint narration for best emotional impact.
- Childish indiscretions to confuse plot, maybe as / when / if old secrets are revealed?
- Dangle the bait for dramatic scenes through rural superstitions/beliefs e.g. witch's prophesies.
- Characters to grow and mature within plot to the point where love story is resolved.

In all these plot thoughts there is no hint of it being a romantic novel *per se*. A family saga built around some kind of industry involves more than a simple love story. Even so, the love story of two strong main characters would be at the heart of the whole plot, but there had to be plenty of tensions, conflicts and misunderstandings before it was resolved, complicated by their opposing families.

It would all be set against an authentic background with believable events, and the kind of characters who were the backbone of that particular lifestyle.

The vague plot outline

Now I needed to gather up everything I knew about the area. I had plenty of maps at home, and a dozen or more of the little holiday booklets I had collected over the years.

My booklets included information about famous wrecks; witchcraft and mystery, Cornish myths and legends, tales of the Cornish wreckers (which I had used for information in my first ever historical romance many years before), Cornish folklore, the coastline of Cornwall, and so on. But shock, horror ... I had absolutely nothing about china-clay, its workings, its lay-out, or its people.

Using your library

I always tell students to make a friend of their local librarians, telling them you are a writer and the kind of research information you need.

My local library supplied everything available on china-clay, and I discovered that there had been a thriving china-clay industry in the 19th century, but it was also an industry of highly fluctuating fortunes. *Great.* There had been many strikes, large ones and smaller ones confined to individual pits. There were disputes galore over the way the clay was transported through St Austell to the port of Charleston, where the streets were regularly covered in white dust from the twice-yearly race through the town of the loaded clay wagons. *Great* again for local colour and authenticity.

Women, men and boys worked at the pits. The women were known as bal maidens, whatever their ages. There was a great divide between the clay bosses and the workers, and there were the in-betweens, the Pit Captains. And to an imaginative writer, here was not only a solid clay background, but in terms of novel potential, pure gold.

I also needed to learn about the methods and workings of a Cornish clay-pit. Cornwall was within reasonable access, and it was no hardship for me to revisit it many times, checking where I wanted my fictional places to be, visiting the China Clay Heritage Centre for more detailed research, and photographing the vast lay-out of a china-clay pit.

Choice of main characters and names

Vague ideas now had to be more specific, involving two families. On one side the boss and his son and several other relatives; on the other, a large family of clayworkers, including a spirited daughter who would be my central character – the pivotal character in the book.

As my plot thoughts evolved, I scribbled them down with question marks beside the doubtfuls or possibles. Knowing that there was to be a love story threaded through the novel, the two main characters were definites.

But what to call them? And what would be the name of the clay works? Until those things were established, none of it would start to be real to me.

I went back to my memories of Cornish names. In old Cornwall the name Killigrew was an important and influential one, and sounds strong and authoritative. Killigrew seemed the perfect choice for my clay works, and when I hit on the book's title, there was an alliteration about it that I loved.

Killigrew Clay ... so this also had to be the name of the owners in the big house, the Killigrews. The son was Ben, simply because the names went smoothly together. Ben Killigrew. And Morwen Tremayne ...

Morwen sounded so beautifully Cornish that she had to be the heroine. Tremayne is essentially Cornish too. She would live with her parents and four brothers in a cottage at the top of the moors, where they could see the stars through the slates. Every member of her family worked at Killigrew Clay, where she and her mother were bal maidens.

I made detailed character profiles of Ben and Morwen and the other important subsidiary characters. In an intricate plot of this kind, involving sub-plots and multi-viewpoints, there were many family members who would take prominent roles throughout the book, and I had to get to know them. I made a provisional 'cast-list', which was added to as and when someone else came into the plot during the actual writing.

I also took care with these lists to avoid characters with similar names or initials.

Where to begin?

Having set up the main characters and the background, the plot had to begin at a dramatic point to bring the readers into my world and introduce them to Ben and Morwen. My research gave me part of the answer. It would be one of the bi-annual charges through St Austell with the clay wagons, a rip-roaring scene of action and danger, and with the more saintly townswomen showing distaste at these lusty clayworkers.

So how and why would my two central characters be involved in such a scene? I decided that Ben would have just returned to Cornwall from his college education and be in St Austell with his father. Morwen would be in the town, buying fruit buns for the family tea, since it was her seventeenth birthday.

Laying clues

This told the readers two things. Ben was an educated young man –and if buying fruit buns was the extent of their daughter's birthday celebrations, then the Tremayne family were far humbler. But in the hurly-burly of the town's excitement at watching the precarious progress of the clay wagons, they accidentally bumped into one another, and Ben's pearl tie-pin scratched Morwen's face.

His father, Charles Killigrew, recognised one of his young bal maidens, and when she blurted out her birthday mission, he magnanimously invited her whole family to Killigrew House for his son's coming-home celebrations. She didn't want to go. Mixing with rich folk wasn't for the Tremaynes ... but she could hardly refuse.

It was an uneasy event for the whole Tremayne family, unused to such grand surroundings and people. Pretty Jane Carrick was obviously very friendly with Ben, and Morwen would feel the first pangs of jealousy. Her dreamy brother Matt would find an unlikely ally in Ben's uncouth cousin, Jude.

The set-up for future conflicts was established, and furthered by the way Morwen later confided in her close friend, Celia Penry. Giving Morwen a confidante was important, and there was huge potential in a sub-plot involving the flightier but more naive Celia, and the earthier Jude Pascoe.

The china-clay industry formed the backdrop of the plot, but the characters were its focal point, and their interactions pushed the plot forward. Morwen believed that Ben was destined to marry Miss 'finelady' Jane, as she disparagingly called her. Jane was better educated than Morwen, better connected, and a better match for the son of a wealthy man.

Problem number 1. But since this was also a 'rags to riches/ Cinderella' story in effect, some way around this had to be found. And just as children rarely marry the people their parents want them to, Ben and Jane had already hatched up a plan of their own, whereby their respective parents thought they were enamoured, when in fact Jane had a lover of her own. Their secret rendezvous were no more than a cover for Jane to meet the brash Yorkshire-born newspaperman Tom Askhew.

The other characters

So what about the other characters in a densely plotted novel of this kind, who were instrumental in the sub-plots?

The large Tremayne family was poor, scratching a living from the clayworks, parents Hal and Bess and their five children. Sam was the eldest, engaged to a local girl. Matt was the dreamer with grand ideas of going to America. Jack just wanted to be like Sam. Morwen was the only girl in the family, beautiful and strong-willed (of course), and the innocent young Freddie provided many of the childish indiscretions indicated above.

Ben's father was widowed, and his housekeeper was his waspish sister, Hannah Pascoe, mother of the objectionable Jude, to whom Charles Killigrew reluctantly gave houseroom.

Sense these people, as I did, solely by their names: Morwen is soft, romantic, mystical; Hannah is tougher, colder; Celia, soft, malleable; Jane, neutral, and any way I defined her; Bess, Morwen's mother, is countrified. And Zillah – Cornish, mysterious, a hard name, a witch's name.

And the men: the name Ben is more neutral than aggressive, but still strong (think of Ben Nevis); Charles, noble by implication; Hal, Morwen's father, countrified. The Tremayne sons, Sam and Jack, have names applicable to their country status; Matt the dreamer is less forceful than the full Matthew; Freddie's lengthier name makes him a pet, a child. Tom Askhew is harder, more aggressive, stamping him as a Yorkshireman in a hard trade, that of newspaperman.

All these demonstrated the way I felt about these characters, and also the way I wanted my readers to see them, without being gimmicky.

Morwen's confidante, Celia Penry, was an essential character in many ways. She was flighty and pretty, and had already caught the eye of the earthy Jude Pascoe at Truro Fair – a useful local tradition for rich colour and description and getting plenty of people together.

Celia was a natural for egging Morwen on to visit old Zillah, the witchwoman who lived in a hovel on the moors (plenty of unpleasant, scary descriptions, set against the mysterious misty moorland atmosphere) in order to get a love potion to see who they would marry.

They had instructions to walk around the old Larnie Stone at midnight, and looking through the hole in its middle, they would see the faces of their true loves.

And wouldn't you just know it? Having learned of the plan from Celia's reckless talk after being plied with too much sweetdrink at Truro Fair, Jude persuaded his cousin Ben to be on the moors at midnight, and this 'accidental' meeting resulted in two things.

Morwen and Ben experienced their first tender feelings for one another. And the teasing Celia was raped by Jude.

NB: Contrasting senses and shock reactions can create the strongest and most emotionally charged scenes.

Scope for surprises

So what happened next? The action was deliberately held up while the clayworkers' plight was detailed, with a march to the offices at St Austell as they demanded higher wages. Personality clashes between violent men demand strong dialogue which had to be used accordingly. No clayworker in the height of his rage would say 'Oh bother' ...

The fury over the clayworkers' demands was left largely unresolved, as Charles Killigrew swore that he wouldn't be browbeaten by his minions. Strikes were threatened and the action was suspended still further.

NB: In such vigorous scenes never be tempted to be held back by your own inhibitions. It's the 'worrying about Auntie Flo syndrome ...' Get over it.

Meanwhile ... time had moved on sufficiently for Celia Penry to discover she was pregnant. Terrified and ashamed, she and Morwen begged Zillah to give her another potion, to rid her of what Zillah called 'the waste'. This resulted in Celia aborting the baby and the two girls burying it on the moors. But the agony and shame of it all turned Celia's mind, with the result ... but wait ...

Meanwhile ... Matt Tremayne and Jude Pascoe had become close, and when Matt returned home one night after a heavy drinking session with his new buddy, he saw something in the milky clay pool, and discovered the body of Celia Penry.

Petrified at what he found, and not knowing what else to do, he took Celia to the Tremayne cottage to consult his sister, and a new nightmare began as Morwen saw the dead body of her friend in her brother's arms.

Throwing curves

But although Morwen knew the reason for Celia's suicide, it threw the superstitious community into unease and uproar. It turned her against Ben, because of his relationship with Jude. It turned her against her beloved brother Matt, because of his continuing friendship with the man who had caused her friend to kill herself.

Then came a localised influenza epidemic, a near-fatal disease in those days. By now Hal Tremayne had been made Pit Captain and the family had moved from the cottage to a small house. And the ailing Charles Killigrew had discovered Morwen's healing hands and suggested she visited him often, rather than have the company of his quarrelsome sister Hannah. Morwen agreed reluctantly, and when Ben succumbed to the disease, he came out of it to find the vision of Morwen Tremayne tending him.

But going up in the world for the Tremaynes did nothing to allay the suspicions and antagonisms of bosses and clayworkers. Ben and Morwen seemed estranged, even when she discovered the truth about his 'arrangement' with Jane Carrick and Tom Askhew. It was still a case of 'them' and 'us', and right then, Morwen wasn't sure to which side she belonged.

Lightening the gloom

But not everything had to be gloom and doom, for heaven's sake, although regional novels do lean towards the dramatic and gloomy side. In every family there are good times and bad – and Sam Tremayne was to marry his long-time love, Dora.

As a counterpoint to this softer episode, Jude Pascoe tried to seduce Morwen, only to have her threaten to expose him over Celia's death if he tried anything on with her again.

Morwen told Ben her suspicions, causing a furious confrontation between him and Jude. Ben was also warring with his father over his wish to build rail tracks from the

130

pit to the port, for the twice-yearly delivery of the clay blocks. This was a pointer to the future after Charles died, when Killigrew Clay came under Ben's control.

NB: These events didn't actually occur until the sequel, and was only an idea for future development and to increase the clayworkers' respect for Ben.

Meanwhile ... When Jude and Matt were in one of their drinking bouts, Jude had also dangled the bait of wrecking and the rich pickings from it, to the gullible Matt. Danger ahead, or what? Logical or not? Was this a likely turn of events?

Wrecking certainly was, with frequently broken and battered ships along the wild Cornish coast. And would these two men get involved? Of course, given their characters, one weak, one strong. And by now, readers were well aware of them. So what outcome did I devise? Remember Matt's dream of going to America? Remember Jude Pascoe's dread of discovery over Celia now and his wild, violent nature? And, as so often happened, a man was killed during the wrecking activities (scope for plenty of authentic description here) and when Jude and Matt were suspected of the crime they panicked and left on a ship bound for America.

Towards resolution

So that got rid of them. But what of the clayworkers and their need for better pay and conditions, and the unresolved love story of Morwen and Ben?

Morwen was strong enough to stand up to Charles Killigrew and tell him of the clayworkers' and her family's troubles. She emphasised Ben's wish to build rail tracks, but her interference only incensed the old man.

In desperation she confided all this to her father – and a small eavesdropper was listening and reported all he knew to the clayworkers ...

And this paragraph is from the text:

He [Freddie] howled as the rest of them set on him, finding himself beneath a tangle of arms and legs. A circle of white, clay-grimed moon-faces loomed above him and threatened to tear his breeches off him and tan his arse if he didn't tell immediately what he knew. And Freddie, as always, gave in.

This situation was the perfect set-up to produce big scenes among the clayworkers; between Ben and Morwen when he discovered she had gone running to her father; and resulting in a bitter strike, with families set against one another, and Morwen's loyalties divided. She left her new employment at Killigrew House and went home. Any happy ending to the love story between her and Ben seemed remote. But wait ...

Bringing in a new twist

As the hero, Ben couldn't be seen as a wimp. Defying his father, he enlisted the unlikely help of the Yorkshireman Tom Askhew (remember him?) who printed a piece in his newspaper about the skinflint Charles Killigrew, and that if other pits in the area began offering more money to these skilled workers, Killigrew Clay would simply die.

The shock of what he saw as his son's betrayal gave Charles a stroke. Morwen seemed to be the only one to calm him. But Ben was the heir to Killigrew Clay, and in the class system of the day, the likelihood of Charles's death would send them poles apart.

Earlier, as a bit of light relief to the plot (thank heavens, I hear you say) young Freddie had persuaded

Morwen to visit old Zillah ... only to be told of an earthquake to come, which Morwen pooh-poohed, but could never quite forget. There were no earthquakes in Cornwall ... everything seemed to be at a standstill, waiting ...

The autumn clay loads were idling at the pits, with no workers willing to take them to Charleston port, until some blacklegs took matters into their own hands, loading them badly onto the waggons and down the steep hills through St Austell, until the loads shifted ...

The prophesied earthquake was not a literal one, but in Morwen's mind it fitted the prophecy, and the effect of the disaster, demolishing buildings in the town, and killing townsfolk and clayworkers, was just as devastating.

Knowing the Killigrews could lose everything through their short-sightedness, Ben now gambled everything and bought out the half-partnership in Killigrew Clay from his father's silent business partner. Faced with his son's stronger character and knowing his own mortality, Charles signed the remaining ownership over to him.

Now Ben faced the angry and mistrusting clayworkers at a town meeting, and informed them of his plans to build rail tracks for the clay transportation. This declaration turned the tide, and showed Ben up in a new and forceful light to those who had doubted his strength.

The strike ended with the promise of more realistic wages and bonuses, and the clayworks was once more in full production. And after much argument and discussion, but finally with parental blessings on all sides, the way was open for Ben and Morwen to find their own destiny and the novel ended with their wedding.

And that might have been the end of their story, but for the sequel ... and the next ...

Summary

- The plot of any novel needs highs and lows.
- Dramatic scenes need their calming counterparts.
- Characters must be consistent while being capable of following new directions when situations demand it.
- Longer novels can support more multi-viewpoints and sub-plots than shorter ones.
- To sustain the interest, hold up the action where possible. Remember TV soap opera techniques.
- Family sagas involve many variations within the characters. Exploit these differences.
- Family sagas inevitably involve tragedies as well as dramatic situations and happy occasions. Don't be afraid of them.

And finally ...

Killigrew Clay was intended as a single novel. But just as in crime novels where an author sees the potential of writing more books about a strong, reader-friendly central character, the ideas for a sequel wouldn't leave me alone. The pointers were all there. The rail tracks were to be built. The Tremayne family had other members whose stories could be told, interwoven with that of Morwen and Ben. I couldn't waste them.

There are eight novels in the Clay series, covering the time from 1850 to the end of the second world war.

N.B. Rowena Summers has long been my pen-name for Cornish and other West Country novels, but more recently I have used the name Rachel Moore for wartime and post-second-world-war sagas set in Cornwall.

10

THINKING COMMERCIALLY

And another book was opened which is the book of life
Revelation

You may think the above quote from the Bible is pretentious in a commercial book of this kind, but it also illustrates exactly what novels are all about. Novels are about life, and the characters you have created to live that life.

It is very heady to decide for the first time that you are going to write a novel. Whatever age that decision comes, it makes no difference to the adrenalin rush it can produce in you – and there have been many instances of first-time novelists making it in later life.

There is no barrier to the age at which a novelist begins to write. It can stimulate your brain, produce new ideas, new experiences, interests and friends.

But regrettably, in this harsh, commercial world, it may make a difference as to whether or not you get published. Publishers like their authors to be 'promotable' these days, and to be an ongoing author. If they suspect that you are on your last legs and may never produce another book, they may be cautious about taking you on. Depressing, isn't it? So what do you do? Lie about your age? Send in a photo that's 25 years out of date for the book jacket? And haven't we all seen *those*...

Being a page-turner

The answer to all this is to produce a book that is so good, so page-turning – that favourite buzz-word of guaranteed success – that no publisher is going to turn it down.

Being a page-turner is something we should all aspire to, and be conscious about, while we are creating our plot and then putting that plot into action during the writing. Being a page-turner is what we would all like to see hyped about us by some unknown critic or enthusiastic publisher's publicity person, in glossy magazines or national newspapers, or on hoardings at railway stations or airports. We wish. I wish ...

But dreaming aside, it all comes down to the nitty-gritty of producing a story that makes readers not only want to keep turning the pages, but makes them *desperate* to do so in order to see what happens next.

To be deserving of the tag of page-turner, that need comes first from within ourselves. When we sort out the final sequence of the plot from the muddle that began in our heads, we must first have that burning desire to know what is going to happen to the characters that we have created.

Our own passion and faith in our plot is what must steer those characters through all the hazards, the disasters, the terrors, the erotic encounters *et al.* that we have intended for them. They must be as important to us as our closest and dearest friends – or even closer.

In effect they are our *alter egos*, and we must *care* what happens to them. Above all else, I think this intimate knowledge of the characters, their past, present and future, is what pushes the plot forward and makes it a page-turner in the eyes of both the publisher and the reading public.

Keeping the readers reading

By now you might well be saying, 'Hey, all I really wanted to do was write a book, without all this formulaic plotting stuff.'

Quite true, and if you can do it, good for you. Starting with one brilliant sentence, and one dynamic character in mind, has produced many a good book – for those who choose to work that way. In any case, all successful novels evolve out of each incident arising naturally out of what has gone before, and if that first scintillating sentence sets you off on a logical train of thought, all well and good.

But for the tentative beginner who is seeking advice on the plotting process, and is stumped at the first hurdle, then in order to keep your readers reading, there are endless questions you should be asking yourself. They may not even occur to the average book-buyer, but will make all the difference as to whether your book gets published at all.

- Take another look at the opening scenes of your book and where your plot really begins to take off. If someone else had written it, would that opening get your attention – and hold it? Is it strong enough to make you want to read on and find out more?

- Your story should have a focus. Remember the readers' expectations in buying this book, and keep your focus in sight. That is, don't change from writing a romantic novel to a science fiction halfway through, or switch from crime to erotica without warning. Readers buy books for entertainment, to be swept away into another world, whether of horror or fantasy or romance; to be informed, amused, educated, inspired, aroused to passion or excitement or fear. *But preferably not all at the same time*!

- Does your plot carry the readers along by a sense of drama, conflict, action and suspense? Has anything significant actually happened between the first page and the last? If not, you don't have a plot, just a meandering series of incidents.

- Look again at your ending. Are you sure it will leave the readers satisfied and think that they have spent an enjoyable time and good money on this book?

Who do you know best?

If you transpose that tired old cliché of writing about what you know to writing about *who* you know ... I can almost hear the answer to the question I have posed. *Myself,* of course!

It's already been said that many people think their own life story would make a fascinating story for others to read. Maybe it would. But who are you? If your name is Idi Amin, or Tony Blair, or Margaret Thatcher, or Gloria Hunniford – or any one of the scores of prominent actors or musical stars – or anyone else on the world stage, then it probably would.

If you are Joe or Jane Bloggs, be realistic and ask yourself who cares about your story. Who is going to pick up an autobiographical book with your name on it and pay money for it? It's a brutal fact of life that no publisher is going to waste money on promoting an unknown. In the commercial sense, the autobiography of the unknown is never going to be an option.

But since it's habitually tossed around that everybody has a story in them, if you are desperate to use your own life story as a plot, then fictionalise it as I have already described. Change the names. Preferably change all or some of the plot, because as sure as the sun rises every morning (British weather permitting), much of your life story is going to be dull, dull, dull ... and if you are going to detail every bit of it, which the novice autobiographer can't resist ... you may as well transmit it straight to the waste bin.

Unless, of course, you're writing it all out for the benefit of your own family, which is a different matter entirely, and something to be highly recommended, in my opinion. I frequently say in any talk I give on research, that once your forbears die a large part of their past – and *your* past – dies with them.

For instance ... I don't know how my Scottish grandfather came to be the Waterworks Manager in Lymington, Hampshire – or how my father, by then living in Somerset, came to meet and marry my mother, a Londoner. None of that older generation is left now to tell me the details, and I would dearly love to know how it all came about.

A personal autobiography written purely for family interest is fine –and a very desirable thing to do – but that is not what we are talking about here, so back to the plot.

It can be a more dangerous game than you imagine to write about yourself and your family and acquaintances, if you are intending it for publication as a kind of factual/fiction book because, inevitably, you involve those other people.

Unless you have lived in a vacuum, you are bound to mention them to a greater or lesser degree. Some may be flattered, but others definitely won't be. You've heard the phrase 'the names have been changed to protect the innocent'.

In fictional terms, you could change that to 'the names have been changed to protect yourself from the enraged, the furious, the scandalised, the solicitors' letters'.

But don't overlook the fact that it's perfectly possible to use the core of your family background, utilising the germ of the ideas and the scope of that unique history to create a work of fiction. It's been done many times, and it's far safer to turn things around than to upset an eccentric aunt by using a name that's too similar to her own, or describing her *faux pas* in intimate detail, which you may not be able to resist.

You may think fondly of her, and that you're doing her a favour by immortalising her but, like Queen Victoria, she is unlikely to be amused. While I frequently suggest that if you find characterisation difficult, you use prominent people or pictures in magazines as role models, there is a fine line to be drawn in taking the essence of those people, and not caricaturing them. Especially your own relatives!

Playing it safe

So what do I mean by turning things around in using your own family background as a starting point for your plot? The most obvious thing is to turn your sleepy little backwater hamlet into a raving city nightspot. Or making your Scottish island setting an Italian resort, or inventing an entirely fictitious island instead of your childhood family holiday venue.

It could be that the eccentric aunt of fond memory could quite usefully be transposed into a fictional teenager, with all the quirkiness of the original. The dour uncle could be the fictional ratty clergyman of the parish. (Some are!) The fictional gossipy village shopkeeper could step right out of your cousin's persona. The weird farm labourer could be a facsimile of the so-called friend of the family who always made you feel slightly creepy as a child.

Maybe he had more than a natural cuddling interest in a small girl that you could never quite understand at the time, and didn't quite like – but put him in a different role and setting, and you have a new and more sinister character, written with all an adult's perception and understanding.

Use all your ingenuity and lateral thinking when creating your page-turning characters, and realise that looking for role models can often mean looking inwards instead of outwards. They are all there for the taking, but also be aware that a heavy disguise is far better than having some angry relative accusing you of putting them in your book.

Funny, you'd think they'd be pleased, wouldn't you? They won't, unless they're the heroes. Even then, if they recognise themselves, they'll tell you that they would never have done this, or *that,* and certainly not the *other* ... no, in my opinion, you're far better off keeping 'em out.

Thinking globally

Think of sex 'n' shopping novels. Think international best-sellers. Think of any glamour-based novels whose plots span continents and sweep readers along from England to France and across the Atlantic to New York and San Francisco. Think of novels that don't keep characters in one small town, but cover a wider canvas, involving the rich, the famous and infamous.

It is obvious that there is a huge market for novels set outside Britain, involving characters we wouldn't expect to meet in our everyday lives. Being realistic again, if you are one of the big names in fiction (and if you are, you won't need to be reading this), then it won't matter where you set your book. Nor will it matter if you are hopefully setting up a new series for yourself – maybe with a fictional detective, or call-girl, or whoever – in your preferred small town.

But if you want to appeal to the vast American and worldwide readership, then a beginner might seriously think more globally than plotting a book set in the wilds of deepest Somewhereshire. And yes, this takes us back to research, into checking the idioms of different-speaking people, accurate place-names and settings, and getting it right.

Publishers are commercial to their finger-tips, and so should you be. So no matter how much time you need to spend on research, or how diffident you are initially at tackling a wider subject for your plot, it will be worth it in the end, because more sales will be the result. And in the hard-hearted business end of publishing, sales are what count.

Popular and saleable plots

But rather than frightening you off, and making you wonder if such plots are beyond you, there's no doubt that there is a consistent place in readers' hearts for home-grown plots of the regional variety. Fiction set in Cornwall, Liverpool, London's East End, and practically every corner of the British Isles, has its faithful following, whatever the genre.

Readers love the familiarity of the kind of characters who inhabit the Yorkshire Dales or the Welsh hills, or the claustrophobic atmosphere of almost any English village, and can seemingly never have enough of them. It makes commercial sense to capitalise on this – until the day comes when publishers, or the mysterious beings who oversee such things, decide that enough is enough, and they want no more.

This happens with most fiction but, thankfully, it is generally temporary. You will hear that Westerns are out. 'Women in jeopardy' plots were hugely popular, then began to fade. The Aga Saga bandwagon was overdone. Medical romances, save for Harlequin Mills & Boon and some Scarlet romances, virtually disappeared. How long will currently popular thirty-somethings humour last?

It's a strange, and constantly infuriating phenomenon, that although we are often told that Historicals are out of favour, the number of historical mini-series on television continues to grow. Publishers may argue that these are the classics, and have a ready viewing audience. Readers will argue that these are stories they want to see and read, as librarians will testify all too readily.

But a historical novel with swashbuckling characters and a densely plotted story will find a home, won't it ...?

Maybe so, if the above requirements are as truthfully portrayed as all that! It still depends very much on publishers and editors, who have their individual voices too. I would always advise you to check what's currently in vogue before you embark on any obscure period of history. *Maybe* there's room for another *Credo,* set in the Dark Ages, and *maybe* the Vikings are due for a revival, but to embark on anything so far out of the norm would always be questionable.

If you spend your time and creative energy on writing a novel, you want that novel to sell. And once you have that book in print, you have a commercial investment for yourself and your publisher. And for your agent too, if you have one.

A published book is a commodity, like anything else. It does not have to end its life with the first publication.

Some do, but let's hope for better things. Let's hope for hardback and paperback sales; for large print and foreign rights; for audio tapes and reprints; for US sales; and for the annual Public Lending Right payments to swell our bank balances.

Not all of those extras will come everyone's way, but the possibilities are within reach of us all, which is what makes writing such an exciting business to be in. Just never lose sight of the fact that it *is* a business, like any other, and that you are your own best salesman – as opposed to those publishers' salespeople who tote your book around to the bookstores in the hope of promoting it.

The best way you can promote yourself is to write a novel that has a solid and well-constructed plot that is visually pleasing and logically sound. A plot that involves characters who leap off the pages and into readers' hearts, because they are believable and realistic, with human faults and virtues.

Above all, the characters are survivors of all that you put them through. They behave consistently, true to themselves, but they will always be developing and maturing as they reach the satisfying end of their story.

To re-cap ...

Constructing the plot before you begin your novel may seem like fumbling your way through a maze. It may seem like far too mechanical a process, when you are itching to get on with the writing. It may seem like far too much work. You may only do half of it before you begin the book. Like me, you may not do the final, detailed plotting before you have actually begun. Or you may constantly revise, tinkering and fiddling with scenes until you are utterly bored with the whole thing and think longingly of taking up a proper job again ...

But it will give you a great and glorious feeling of achievement when you have sorted out that rambling, sketchy outline into some kind of order; when you know your characters inside out and what motivates them; when you have planned the major incidents, if not all the smaller ones, that will enhance and enrich the narrative.

You are finally on your way. Of course, you've still got to write the damn thing ... and there is still the little matter of the synopsis. Oh – you thought you'd done that?

Maybe you have. But remember that you may find it far easier to plot the entire outline in detail, and then condense it into the bare essentials – the synopsis. It's your choice.

If you have constructed the detailed plot for your own guidance, and you plan to write the entire novel and send it to an agent or publisher, then you may not even feel the need for a synopsis. The great advantage of it, though, is that you can see the overall shape of the plot in a nutshell.

If you plan to send the first three chapters only, then you definitely *do* need to send a synopsis with that material, so that the editor knows what the book is all about, from beginning to end. Which is where we came in.

Summary

- Plot your novel to appeal to the widest readership.
- Keep your autobiography for family reading.
- Whatever you write, be passionate about it.
- Remember you are in the entertainment business.

REFERENCES

Author's Works Referred to in This Book
All in the April Morning
Ashton's Folly (writing as Jean Innes)
The Bannister Girls, W. H. Allen / HarperCollins / Macmillan
A Gentleman's Masquerade (writing as Sally Blake), Harlequin Mills & Boon
Killigrew Clay (writing as Rowena Summers), Severn House
Primmy's Daughter (writing as Rowena Summers), Severn House
Scarlet Rebel, Severn House / Macmillan / Ballantine
To Love and Honour
Willow Harvest (writing as Rowena Summers), Severn House
Wives, Friends and Lovers, Robinson Scarlet

Recommended Resources
Leslie Dunkling, *The Guinness Book of Names*
Patrick Robertson, *The Shell Book of Firsts*, Ebury Press
Jean Saunders, *How to Research Your Novel*, Allison & Busby
Jean Saunders, *The Craft of Writing Romance*, Forward Press
Jean Saunders, *How to Write Realistic Dialogue*, Forward Press
Jean Saunders, *How to Create Fictional Characters*, Forward Press

Website
www.jeansaunders.net

INDEX

For more information about our books please visit

www.accentpress.co.uk